NOT DEAD YET

An Anthology of Survivor Poetry

Penhall Publishing

2014

ISBN 978-0-9897893-4-9 Color Edition
978-0-9897893-6-3 Black & White Edition
978-0-9897893-5-6 Electronic Book

Cover design by Lilly Penhall, Interstellar Graphics
Front cover photo by Rosie Lindsey
Back cover photos: "New Growth" by Chuck Taylor, "Skin Deep" by TM Rhyno, "Heart Energy" by Maranda Russell, and "Blue" by A Nero
Penhall Publishing logo designed by Eileen Simeonov

Previously Published Works:

PW Covington: "Short Final (Somalia 1992-93)" appeared in his collections *Like the Prayers of an Infidel...* and *I Did Not Go Looking for This.*
Jennifer Hudgens: "Any Good" appeared in *Light as a Feather* by Swimming with Elephants Publications, 2014.
Claire Ibarra: "C'est La Vie" appeared in Counterexample Poetics, January 2014.
Agnes Marton: Travelmarvel: appeared in Danse Macabre
Exposed: appeared on Michelle McGrane's poetry blog *Peony Moon* as a part of protest 'Against Rape'
Lilly Penhall: "Today" & "Scars" appeared in her collection *O* by Penhall Publishing.
James Barrett Rodehaver: "i love you like burning churches still pray" and "ode to tortured artist" appeared in his collection *Strangely Wonderful* by Penhall Publishing
Sharon Sitler: "Abuse" appeared in 2013 edition of *Paper Nautilus.*
Bekah Steimel:
"She's a pure personality" appeared in *Brickplight*, May 2014.
"When I needed traction the most" appeared in *One Sentence Poems*, May 2014.
"Does it get any better than this" appeared in *Too Much: An Anthology About Excess* from Unknown Press, July 2014.
"My fear of heights..." appeared in *Thirteen Myna Birds*, January 2014.
"Here I am again..." appeared in *Verity La*, Oct. 2013.
"Today I fished..." appeared in *TRIVIA: Voices of Feminism*, Fall 2013.
"How could I..." appeared in *RiverLit*, No. 8.
Edward Vidaurre: "How to watch me wither" appeared in his collection *Insomnia.*

"No matter what people tell you,
words and ideas can change the world."

— Robin Williams (1951 - 2014)

#contents

#foreword by Todd "Grendel" Pack   11
Introduction by Chuck Taylor   15

#broke   **17**
Photo by Rosie Lindsey   18
Wal-Mart Land by Maranda Russell   19
Autopsy. by Jennifer E. Hudgens   20
Beautifully Broken by Jerri Hardesty   21
Dribble, Deities Haunt Hallways. by Jennifer E. Hudgens   26
Hangin' at Joe's Hole by Rose M. Smith   27
i love you like burning churches still pray... by James Barrett
Rodehaver   28
Metal Dragon. by Jennifer E. Hudgens   30
"Skull Study" by TM Rhyno   31
Mother, may I? by Evan Bryant Patton   32
Pawn Shop by Sharon Sitler   33
Pyrrhic Victory by Adam Eason   34
Sick and Tired by Travis Laurence Naught   36
Photo by Rosie Lindsey   38
O, Beautiful by Todd "Grendel" Pack   39

#familycrisis   **43**
Painting by A Nero   44
Underwater House by Alex Pogosov   45
Broken Mends by Christopher Johnson   49
Old Father, Old Artificer by Evan Bryant Patton   52
Unboxed by Heather M. Browne   55
Death is not the Problem, Death is the Solution by Evan
Bryant Patton   56
Scrubbing by Heather M. Browne   58
"Watching Over Me" by Claire Ibarra   59
I've lived in that house. by James Barrett Rodehaver   60

Silent Dog by Paul Koniecki   64
being supportive by Ricky Pursley   67
For Andreas by Susan Dobbe Chase   68
Painting by A Nero   69

#calamities   **71**
Painting by A Nero   72
Absolute Entity by Aparna Pathak   73
Firefighters. by Terri Richardson   74
The Last Time That The World Ended by PW Covington   75
Twisting and Turning by Allison Bruning   77
"Facing the Storm" by Maranda Russell   78
"Ours is not to wonder why…" by Stephen Lawson   81
Connect the Wild Dots by Paul Koniecki   83
Short Final (Somalia 1992-93) by PW Covington   86
You Take From Me by Heather Browne   88
Static by WC Chambers   90
Painting by A Nero   93

#lovegonewrong   **95**
"Sanguine Slavery" by TM Rhyno   96
Exposed by Agnes Marton   97
Our Penny by Heather M. Browne   98
On Instinct: Found Love notes by Jennifer E. Hudgens   99
"C'est la vie" by Claire Ibarra   100
Attempted Murder of a Love Life by Yocelin Watts   101
Spiraling by Tavis P. Brunson   103
Abuse by Sharon Sitler   106
Simple Confession by Trier Ward   107

#scars   **111**
"Heart Energy" by Maranda Russell   112
a letter to me from my scar by D. Victory   113
Far Away. by Eric Blackerby   115
Sweet Waltz. by Jennifer E. Hudgens   116

battleground. by James Barrett Rodehaver 117
Breast monologue by Lori Lasseter Hamilton 118
Scar-light. by Jennifer E. Hudgens 120
Deaf Couple by Emma van Woerkom 121
Scars by Lilly Penhall 122
Any good. by Jennifer E. Hudgens 123
Welcome to the show by Lori Lasseter Hamilton 124
Photo by Rosie Lindsey 125
a million kisses and a comet's tail to the edge of the milky way by
Paul Koniecki 127
Troubles by WC Chambers 129
pretty in pink by Lori Lasseter Hamilton 133
Photo by Rosie Lindsey 135

#trauma **139**
"Skin Deep" by TM Rhyno 140
Cry by D. Victory 141
forgiveness Christopher Johnson 144
Drawing by Alex Pogosov 148
Move Slow by Justin Booth 149
Communion by Evan Bryant Patton 152
Precipitation by Johnny Olson 154
A Perfect Storm by Jerri Hardesty 158
Open Letter: I Will Rename Us by Gayle Bell 160
Ape Bite by Grant Leuning 162
No. by Jennifer E. Hudgens 163
This Poem by Jerri Hardesty 165
Jock Dates Drummer. by Logen Cure 168
Suicide Aftermath by Maranda Russell 169
Today by Lilly Penhall 170
Photo by Rosie Lindsey 173
take your seat please/playground marbles by Paul Koniecki 174
One-Night Fosters by Rose M. Smith 178
Desecrated by Terri Black 180
Monster by Tavis P. Brunson 184

Painting by A Nero   186

#demons   **189**
"American Justice" by TM Rhyno   190
Sometimes a bullet looks pretty good by Desmene Statum   191
Gainful Employment by Brad Wood   192
Five Years. by Eric Blackerby   196
Untitled by Bekah Steimel   197
This One Thing I Pray by Justin Booth   207
Amnesia by Brad Wood   211
Monsters by Christoper Johnson   217
4:22 AM: Tripping on K-Pins by Dan Provost   218
How to watch me wither by Edward Vidaurre   220
May. by Logen Cure   221
Night Roaming. by Eric Blackerby   222
Photo by Rosie Lindsey   223
Coming Early by Paul Koniecki   225
Summers by Justin Booth   228
Cripple by Helen Coy-Gresavage   229
It by Dan Provost   230
Ode To Tortured Artist. by James Barrett Rodehaver   231
Whiskey Psalm. by Jennifer E. Hudgens   235
I'll be out in a minute. by Logen Cure   236
NYD... WNYL? by Coyote Wiley   238
Recidivists by PW Covington   241
Painting by A Nero   242
Unopened Letter by Tavis P. Brunson   244
My Demon by Trier Ward   247
Ode to Cut by Paul Koniecki   248

#phoenix   **253**
Photo by Chuck Taylor   254
Travelmarvel by Agnes Marton   255
Jericho A.D. by Todd "Grendel" Pack   256
The Phoenix by Allison Bruning   258

Untitled by Christopher Johnson 261
They Sicken by Justin Booth 262
Like a Fox by Todd "Grendel" Pack 264
Name by D. Victory 268
Doppler Dreams by Emma van Woerkom 270
It's Gonna Hurt. by James Barrett Rodehaver 271
Twist by Todd "Grendel" Pack 274
Stuffed Animals by Maranda Russell 277
So the Universe Imagines by Melissa R. Root 278
"The Water Drove Her Crazy" by TM Rhyno 279
Thoughts On Healing. by James Barrett Rodehaver 280
Sensei by Coyote Wiley 281
Silence is Disturbing by Todd "Grendel" Pack 285
All There Is. by Terri Richardson 288
Yawn, It's Going To Be A Long Day by Travis Laurence Naught 289
Mirrors by Trier Ward 291
Exercise by WC Chambers 293
In the Flames by Shelley Wallace 299
"Set Free" by Claire Ibarra 300

#aboutthesurvivors **302**
#editors 302
#contributors 304
Notes on the Creation of This Anthology 334

#foreword

Survivor poetry.

Over the past few months, I've been pondering this concept—the basis of this book—and all the ramifications. It's certainly a complex topic, and most people who hear the two words together are going to be scratching their heads. The difficulty in explaining it is not limitation, but the very broadness of it.

Poetry, among the arts, is probably the least likely to raise your profit margins in a strictly financial sense. That being said, most poets I know are quite capable of doing other kinds of "work," quite simply because we HAVE to in order to survive in a world that, for the most part, disregards our art as trivial. That we can do this, and STILL continue to craft wisdom and wit into words, is a testimony to the fact that poets are survivors.

Now, anyone can write poetry. It's true. I believe that poetry is the native tongue of the soul, and part of our birthright. But to be a poet—that is, to define your life's work, your vocation, as the pursuit of poetry—is another thing entirely. It's no life for wimps. I'm telling you this from the perspective of a guy who lived out of the back of an Italian restaurant, working for tips that were mostly spent printing fliers for the local poetry slam. In this book, you're going to encounter poets who've suffered far more restrictive limitations, more dire circumstances, and out of those very adversities hone their poetic craft to razor sharpness.

It would be impossible for me to talk about this subject without referring to the project's editor, affectionately known to most of us as "Bear." As with many modern contacts, Facebook was the medium through which I came to know and respect Bear. He is without a doubt one of the bravest poets I've ever encountered in written or spoken format; he doesn't mince around a topic, he goes to war with it, and comes back with the still-beating heart of the matter in his hands. He's wrestled more than one angel to a draw, not the least of which is the physical limitations imposed on him by his "handicap." That word might cause some to recoil, but not Bear . . . he knows his limitations, and the challenge of overcoming those limitations is exactly what drives him on, what hones his craft.

Those of you who are reading this volume, brace yourselves. Poets are, like most artists, creatures of passion, and tend to experience the cutting edge of human emotion... and they want to TELL you about it! These poems are going to leap off of the page, grab you by the throat, and demand your attention. You may be shocked, offended, amazed, amused—sometimes all at once—but if you weather the wordstorm, you'll gain the advantage of a wider perspective.

A great many of these poets have experience with, or have indulged in, the verbal "sparring" known as poetry slams, an art form pioneered by Chicago poet Marc "So What" Smith. I think sometimes of the disdain leveled at the slam by people (some of whom should KNOW better), as if the poetry slam was some sort of house of ill repute, a bit too tawdry for "respectable" folk. Rest assured, if you read this book, or attend a poetry slam, some of your sacred cows will walk out with bite-marks. If the thought of having to double-check your preconceived notions troubles you, here comes trouble. But if politicians and pundits wanted to find the best social barometer, the way to really keep their finger on the pulse of the nation, they'd spend more time attending poetry slams and open mics, and listening to the voices of these incredible creatures that have survived all along, mostly without their attention.

You want to know how to stretch a 10-hour paycheck to cover two weeks? Ask a poet. Want to know how to create beauty when your own body is at war with you? Ask a poet. Want to know what to do when you're at your wits' end, when it seems as if every 10 minutes of your life is pre-scheduled and every 30 seconds some soundbite or commercial wants to send you screaming into the streets, because whatever they're selling you... just... gotta... HAVE IT, and you don't know how to deal with it... slow down long enough to read this book, or stop in at your local poetry slam or open mic, and get a fresh perspective on surviving the life.

I've heard some say that poetry is dead, or that all poetry is the sole province of dead white guys. But those of us who survive, for and by, this craft, it is our lifeblood, and we're NOT DEAD YET!

Todd "Grendel" Pack

A meteor enters
the outer atmosphere
She begins to smoke and glow
shrinking under the friction
of the mighty air

She is blazing
and wishes to be called
a falling star
but she's not dead yet
no not dead not dead yet

Chuck Taylor

#broke

For those of us beautifully broken, and/or those of us struggling financially. Either way, these poems make it clear that no matter how broke or broken we are, we will never give up, and will always find a way to survive.

Wal-Mart Land

This ain't no fairy tale—
no Snow White
and the seven dwarves
crap.

This is Wal-Mart Land,
the perfect place
for a huntsman on a budget
or a wicked stepmother
in need of beauty aids.

In this world,
poisoned apples
arrive by the truckload
and magic mirrors
make the dwarves look taller.

But happy-ever-afters
are in short supply,
and our princes
have been outsourced
to China.

Maranda Russell

Autopsy.

When crime scene investigators find my body,
limbs resting between a urine stained dumpster,
finally free of worry,
my smile hanging half-cocked same as the moon,
last image burned into retinas, a star I kissed Calliope.

Fingertips worn away,
coroner called me Veronica,
she gathered red dirt from fingernails,
swabbed my lips for any sign of surrender, sweet evidence
photographed wrists, ankles, table,
first incision climbed into my quieted belly.

Cracked my ribcage open, slid her hands in
removed poems buried there,
every organ weighed and measured,
she named my tongue Aphrodite,
cradled my lungs, sang a solemn lullaby
sewed carcass back together,
wept for the canvas it could have been.

She whispered you were loved onto the left earlobe,
pulled a poly-cotton blended bed sheet over skin, feet exposed
signed the toe tag beautiful, fastened it to the dead,
turned off florescent lights hesitantly,
walked down a long hallway,
she exited to find rebirth in the sun.

Jennifer E. Hudgens

Beautifully Broken

They call us poets,
Damaged imperfect vessels
Filled with damaged perfect intentions
And so many holes,
Poetry is forced to seep out.

We are the walking wounded,
Living proof
That if you just keep putting
One foot in front of the other,
You keep moving forward.

But we are so much more than that.

We are all beautifully broken.
See how the light
Splinters into rainbows
As it passes through the cracks.

We are all soiled,
Dirtied by our own hands
Or by those of others,
But what exquisite, spectral
Artwork
Is created from stained glass.

We are geodes
Whose glittering crystalline caverns
Were not revealed
Until we were cut.

We are wheelchair dancers,

Rejoicing in the complexities
Of circles.

We are garbage, refuse,
Left on the curb as trash,
Reassembling ourselves
Into sculptures.

We are the scar
Of the organ donor,
Evidence that something living
Was given from one person
Unto another.

We are the infant, miraculously found
Alive, a survivor amidst
The rubble of war.

We are a tangled thicket
Of thorny weeds
That have learned
To be flowers.

We are agate,
Whose concentric bands
Of shape and color
Were unseen
Until we were sliced.

We are surgeons,
Performing open-heart procedures
On ourselves
Using pens as scalpels,
Trying to repair torn hearts
Using lines of poetry

As sutures.
And we all have our anesthetic of choice.

We have ink in our veins
That only spills
Onto these pages and stages
When we bleed in some way.

We are multi-syllabic words
Pronounced by a two-year-old child,
Who has no idea of their meaning,
Just loves the way they feel
In the mouth,
The musical sound.

We are sand dollars
Opened to let the doves out.

We are explosions on the horizon
From which you cannot avert
Your eyes, though you know
Something's been destroyed there,
But, oh, how brilliantly we blaze
Against the backdrop of night.

We are a broken-winged bird
Rediscovering the sky.

We are big bangs
In which universes collapse
And are recreated.
And we all have someone's bootprints
In the stardust of our past.

We are precious gems,

Rubies and diamonds
Whose sparkling potential
Was hidden
Until we were faceted.

We are shooting stars,
Meteors
Whose sparking arcs
Mark their own demise.

We are a swan dive suicide,
So graceful in our self destruction,
We almost make it look like
Flying.

We are a long lonely note
On a blues guitar
Stumbling drunk out of a smoky bar.

We are train wrecks,
Natural disasters,
Acts of terrorism
That might just cause people to
Stop
And come together
For a second.

We are the grass
That grows through the sidewalk cracks,
We exist,
We persist,
And we will not let our
Off-key symphonies go unnoticed.

I have bathed in the words

Of poet/prophets,
The luminous liquid dripping
From their lips
And seeping into my pores
Until I am translucent.
I have seen them dancing 'round
The bonfires they ignite on stage,
Lost in their own rhythms,
Earthbound angels
Drawing hieroglyphs
With the motion of their hips
Until we all glisten with the listening,
Sacred symbols in our sweat.

Yes, they call us poets,
But it might be more appropriate
Just to call us
Poetry.

Jerri Hardesty

Dribble, Deities Haunt Hallways.

Praying to Annabel, hoping she hasn't forgotten I'm still breathing,
beg her to bring me holy water to sip, to wash my filthy hands in,
humbled at the idea of drinking men dry, so I don't go thirsty
he bruised my collarbone and neck, bent me between his teeth a willing rosary,

beg her to bring me holy water to sip, to wash my filthy hands in,
this city has pulled the fight from my lungs, danced coward in my muscle,
he bruised my collarbone and neck, bent me between his teeth a willing rosary,
wine siphoned remorse from blood, leaves mouths craving another's saliva,

this city has pulled the fight from my lungs, danced coward in my muscle,
humbled at the idea of drinking men dry, so I don't go thirsty,
wine siphoned remorse from blood, leaves mouths craving another's saliva,
praying to Annabel, hoping she hasn't forgotten I'm still breathing.

Jennifer E. Hudgens

Hangin' at Joe's Hole

Months after you died, Rosie downed that bottle
of Lithium like Anne in The Valley[1] but only flirting,
chased an answer to the only question she ever asked herself,
then lay down on my friend Diana's sofa,
arm hung over the edge, pill bottle still in hand.
It was early, but she knew Diana'd find her—maybe
in time, and maybe not.   Days later she confessed
it was a Baptist girl's escape, to lie back,
let death's welcome hands touch
places careless lovers had avoided.

That dose was not enough to kill the rumors
she'd been hanging out at Joe's Hole
and buddy she'd been around. Rosie could count
her suitors on less than a hand, but that no longer mattered
when they placed your face on Main Street
where you imagined all the hoes hung out—
in a little brick building with a name like a vagina
and a signal for a door, and what else
would a Baptist girl think?
But that's what she got for hangin' out
with fast girls who'd been there more than once.

It was days after Cheri sent that man to turn her out
of that DJ's life for good. Nothing takes away
a guilt-ridden sinner's will to live like being told he
heard she slept around, too. So she counted out the pills,
counted them a sweet relief, swallowed them with Coke
to make them act real fast, and prayed she'd either die
or dream that dreadful past away. Some say
it was a miracle that Diana found her.
The paramedics, though, knew there was not a chance
she'd get away from stories quite so easily—on white dolls
bringing relaxation just ten milligrams at a time.

Rose M. Smith

[1]Valley of the Dolls, Jacqueline Susann (Grove Press, 1966)

i love you like burning churches still pray...

i love you like a parked car filled with screaming men,
fighting desperately because they care.
i love you like a one-bedroom apartment filled to the ceiling
with little houses crafted from dreams.
i love you like urgent cafe whisperings about finances and patience,
the occasional muffled shout leaping out despite the crowd.
i love you like my hands around the neck of my pillow,
bashing something that will not break.
i love you like being asked baffling questions
and pressing rudely for the answer why.
i love you like frantic public compromises as shady as backroom deals,
and just as wrong.
i love you like manipulative leading statements and questions
that i puppet to steer things in my favor.
i love you like squeezing your hand in the midst of a fight,
as my stomach climbs up my esophagus and chokes me.
i love you like hot tears run down cheeks,
and into the guilty party's waiting hand.
i love you like how we lie to ourselves, "we're gonna make it,"
and how we tell the truth, "it's not so bad."
i love you like tantrums tumbling around on four wheels,
punching the airbag so hard i expect it to fly out and kill me.
i love you like a child, addicted to being told it'll be okay right?
and we're safe, right? and will you hold me?
i love you like the way we guard the money we don't have,
and the fear of losing it all.
i love you like the way i hate explaining stuff to you,
and love being needed at the same time.
i love you like a fool loves god, fervently and unquestioning, willing to do anything,

and with the belief in resurrection after death due to his love.
i love you like burning churches still pray,
and wounded children still believe in santa.
i love you like a sick man loves the sickness,
and the cure, and the attention.
i love you like a star loves having its space,
and like horses love stars, incomprehensibly yet intimately.
i love you like a barnacle loves whatever it can stick to and survive,
but also like a disease, all i wanna do is get under your skin and change you.
i love you like the poetry you don't get, but somehow can still feel the undertow of,
and stay above water; some depths are not for everyone,
(trust me, you'd be crushed down there.)
i love you like the sappy shit we do because we are a couple,
and the rest of the stuff we do because we are impatient, and hungry, and foolish.
i love you like my incessant pleading for yet another thing we don't need,
currently it's a cat, and my love for you will be all the more when you say no.
i love you like the bedroom laughter that fills our room like smoke,
and suffocates both of us, as we giggle until we cannot breathe, or are we choking?
i love you like the next great thing we will accomplish together,
a sensual mystery teasing us with anticipation, danger, and new challenges.
i love you like my books, and possibly even more; i've piled you boxes high in my apartment,
or stacked some parts of you on my nightstand, just in case i want to do it in bed.
i love you like the blank space beneath these lines, silently and with great hope for the future,
and i know what we write together will be just as great as what i've written alone.

i love you, and there is truly nothing like it.
nothing at all.

James Barrett Rodehaver

Metal Dragon.

Rid me of my zombie ways,
dear one,
if found as corpse,
in a wild white room,
perhaps you will love me then,
my lips turned away from the sky,
eyes a permanent shade of midnight,
holy-crept up the backs of calves,
thighs,
things they will use to identify my body,
3 a.m.

Jennifer E. Hudgens

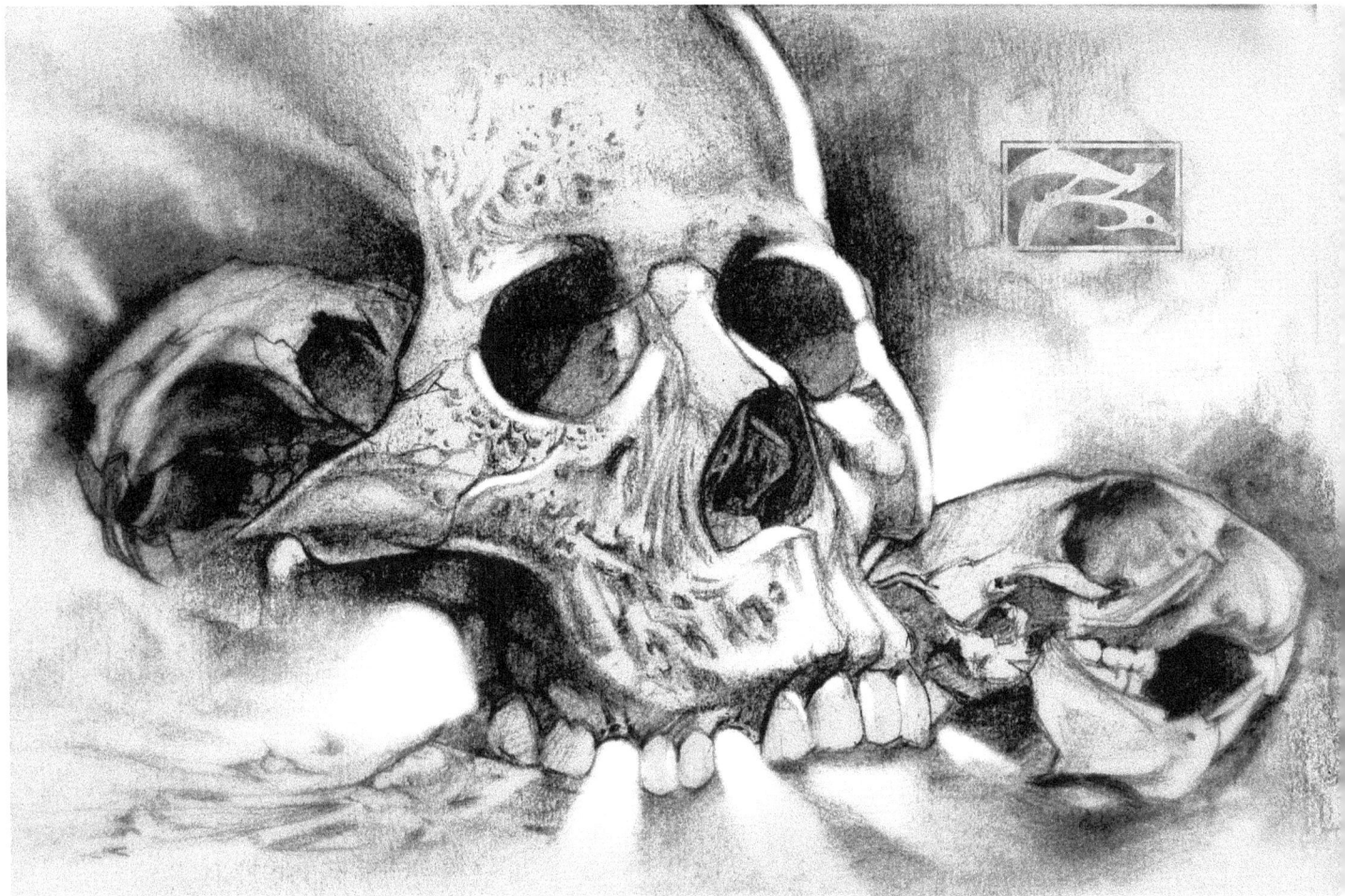

"Skull Study" by TM Rhyno

Mother, may I?

Mother got the pink slip.
Twenty years of working for the red,
white and blue, tired and bruised
carpal tunnel in her elegant wrists
that she uses to dance salsa
in weekend mambo and cumbia dreams

Mother got a new job
retail service at Buckees pit stop,
get your hot dog and 44oz,
race through a checker-flag dawn
while mamasita pumps your gas

Mother told me, these days she's tired,
"I just walk and walk and don't go anywhere,
it's a dead end." My second-generation ears
in-tune with her fractured English,
la migra's tired wrist stroking
her native son's thin, straight, hair

Mother, may I take a job from the state,
while you slave under immigrant name?
Mother are you happy for me?
Mother do I contribute to your oppression?
I've learned my lesson,
red, white, and blue is the way
there is no black and white,
but only grey.

Evan Bryant Patton

Pawn Shop

He counts out a crisp one hundred dollar bill. A twenty. A limp five. He smells like cigarette smoke. A passing ambulance wails. The necklace remains in my hand. I rub a white pearl between my thumb and forefinger. You laughed when I asked for it, when I told you that every girl needs a pearl necklace. You gave me that but you also gave me this. The smooth pearl is harsh in my hands and I recall that when silk snaps it does so silently and things get lost. I surrender the strand. Collect the bills. The bell above the door rings.

Sharon Sitler

Pyrrhic Victory

They cut me open
laid my body bare
seen parts of me
I'll never see
breathing organs
twitching nerves

they found a dead dog
corrupting my spleen
and religion proselytizing
my liver's drunken days,
traffic jam clogged intestines
spewing ozone-laced bile
and a severed ear oppressing my lungs
listening and waiting and bleeding.

My heart was silent smoking,
they said, absent looking
to far off corners in its cell,
a hundred unopened letters
stacked and tied and stamped:

RETURN TO SENDER

My stomach was gestating a pearl,
they said, a clammy orb as big
as a baseball, slipping
layer and layer and glistening
pale stars and clouds,

but they removed it and sold it,
they said, to pay for the surgery.

They cleaned me out best they could,
a cellular diaspora, clamps and cataclysm,
scalpels severing impalpable pieces,
polyurethane gloves probing drug induced dreams,
untying knots and uprooting my life's lineage
then sutured and scarred and sewed me closed.

I woke fingering new faults cracking my torso.
Surgery was a success, they said.

It is true, I think, they evicted my tenants,
but inside, my cindered slums remain.

Adam Eason

Sick and Tired

Early stages of being sick
start with a general feeling of malaise and body weakness,
feelings of faint washing over at inopportune times
like an old man on the dance floor
creeping along in a sea of writhing bodies
trying only for his place of respite
except that a rowdy drunk is standing at the finish line
cavorting with the other men for sips from their pitcher and
he sees a new target to obstinately throw his arms around
congratulatory kind words for favor ...

Shaking that leech off and pressing hard through the night
until the trip home that takes eons opposed to normal minutes
is rewarded by a kind bed that does not allow him to go lonely
through dream filled adventures of revenge murder and sex
spurred on by tumultuous feelings of physical pain
encountered while waking
to reposition in search of a few more fleeting moments
before taking on the next day that contains plans kept,
changed and lacking any major responsibility ...

Allowing discomfort to creep further from the center
throughout all limbs and skin until anxiety begins to build
about whether this is the beginning of the end or
just another swerving part on the road map of a life
that has been on a beautiful straight stretch
save some unmarked potholes that provided excitement
in place of cruise control sailing which appeared to be leading
toward the second star to the right as if in Peter Pan
except those tales only exist in stories,
the hill dropping over into curved territory
remains unseen until the moment gravity is defied

for a split second the brakes are pumped
in realization of sudden danger...

Hope it's not too late kick whatever is trying to take over
because there are uncertain things so invigorating yet to be encountered
it would be a shame to die over something as simple as exhaustion
from trying too hard to take on a life that has been very willing to give
when asked for, deserving to be thanked and appreciated
rather than discouraged or frustrated at
unless all of those negative feelings are verified and
this really is the unequivocal end...

Travis Laurence Naught

O, Beautiful

O, beautiful for spacious skies
filled with toxic gases, for amber waves of
genetically altered grain;
for purple mountain majesties
removed to eke out tons of coal
above the fruited plain
where the trees are cut down
for mini-malls and housing developments
that you can't afford to move into.

America, America,
God shed His grace on you
and you squandered it
to create new & improved
versions of oppression,
and motherhood is a losing game
because your kids, unborn and otherwise,
are all owned by the state
and the corporations that own the state.
You can forget about the crown,
you've lost it while looking down
on everyone that dwelled below
your dollar-sign timberline
that's now owned by China and the Fed.

Speaking of fed, America,
future generations that starve
because you spent their inheritance
for more ways to poison or torture
or just plain kill, well, let's just say
that the lords of creation
will look more like "Lord of the Flies,"

and maggots will feed off their eyes,
because nobody will mourn them
when they die, let alone
take the time to bury them.
You've taken Social Darwinism to a whole new level, claiming
that "achievers" and "job creators" were the most fit to survive,
but when the ones who've labored
so they could dwell in a high-rise
turn on them,they'll be revealed for the
aberrations that they are,
and the many, though small and meek,
will rise to claim their inheritance.

America, the beacon of freedom
is flickering out,
hijacked by politicians and pundits,
pimped on every shore
but our own, proclaiming a nation's glory
but look at the nation's poor
and you'll read another story.
If you continue to squander
the grace that God shed,
there won't be anything left
for you to squabble over.
Remember that line
"the last shall be first, and the first
shall be last?" Well, in case
your head's still stuck up your ass,
that isn't just an allegory.

Todd "Grendel" Pack

#familycrisis

Sometimes those closest to us can be the ones to destroy our trust and hurt us the most. The shock from a family member's betrayal or abuse, or the loss of a loved one, can send us reeling, wounded and guarded into despair. But if we can rise above the pain and the anger, we realize that sometimes, family means those around us who love us most and always build us up. No matter who we must leave behind in our search for true acceptance and love, we will be stronger and wiser for the experience, knowing full well what, and who we survived.

Underwater House

When I was a little kid, I used to have a recurring dream about living in an underwater house. I still remember what it looked like with its dim lamps and maroon couch and dark colored wallpaper. It looked vaguely like a set from a '20s or '30s period film. Sometimes I'd be there with my whole family—Mom, Dad, and Sister, and sometimes I'd be there by myself.
And that scared me.
What didn't scare me, or rather what didn't occur to me, was how I was breathing under water. I lacked, as most five-year-olds do, even a basic knowledge of biology, and I didn't know how to swim yet, so I never had to hold my breath or worry about not inhaling water.
In a house,
Surrounded by my family,
Under water,
I would drown!
And that's basically what happened to my father seven months ago when he died in a hospital bed, surrounded by loved ones, drowning on his own mucus because his body was too weak to cough it up. The doctors didn't attempt to pump it out because we had signed a "do not resuscitate" form, and if this didn't kill him, the metastatic cancer and multiple infections soon would. All we could do was sit and wait and have the doctors continually give him morphine as he slept, waking for a moment now and then to gasp and fade out again to the gurgling sound of the humidifier on the oxygen tank cranked to "10".
I couldn't help but start to breathe in unison with him, but the gasps made me feel weird, and I had to consciously force myself to stop.
I moved to the mattress on the floor, where my sister had slept the previous night. My mom was on the cot, where she had stayed
In his room
For the entire length of his hospitalization and now here, in the

skilled nursing facility.

I pulled my hood over my head to block out the room lights and try to get some rest, but instead, for the first time during this whole ordeal, I cried,

And I asked God a question.

Not in anger and not as a plea but as a request

For an explanation.

I said "What the fuck did you do to my family!?" knowing that my dad would soon be gone, and my sister was on a plane back to Connecticut where she lived with her husband and daughter. Then I felt the heat in my face subside, and I dried my eyes and promised myself that I wouldn't cry again because that necessary part of the process was over, and there would soon be arrangements to make.

I got up to get the nurse to check on my dad, and I went to pee. I exited the bathroom to see the nurse feel his pulse as it faded, and shortly thereafter, she clocked the time of death—2:38 pm.

It sounded almost comforting as she said it,

And she was beautiful,

Tall, brown-skinned, and my same age.

But there's nothing beautiful about death. Forget the Neil Gaiman character. It's all gaping mouth and skin infections, the smell of decay, excrement, yellow skin, and a catheter. And this is the "good" way to die—here, in the expensive nursing home where some loophole in Medicaid allowed my dad to stay. Where ordinarily rich people pay upwards of $200 a day to house their elderly and embarrassingly not self-reliant.

I had a medical mask on as I stood over him and put the pennies on his eyes to pay Charon the ferryman on the river Styx. I did that literally, by the way—the pennies thing is not a metaphor. They were later buried with him, in his suit jacket pocket because I figured he probably wouldn't have liked the idea of them slowly descending into his eye sockets over the coming centuries.

This is the kind of stuff you're not supposed to talk about with people who haven't seen it first-hand. It's like a soldier coming home, having witnessed war atrocities. He never answers the first

"How are you?" coming off the plane with, "Well, I could have done without the whole seeing a child get eviscerated thing." It just doesn't happen.

Back at the nursing home, after comforting my mom (as much as I could in this situation), I got on the phone and called my friend the undertaker. Again, I'm not using some literary device. I'm literally friends with this guy. I have been for years. We hang out sometime, and talk about TV shows, relationships, the usual stuff. He rushes over, does his thing, and then it's on to the signing of forms and the rest of it.

I still think about it.

A lot,

And how

I don't want to go out like that.

That's why I'm aiming for political assassination. I'll get shot in the middle of giving a speech, like Billy Pilgrim in *Slaughterhouse Five*. I'll become a more outspoken anarchist, and one day, when I'm speaking of the merits of a Noam Chomsky-style rejection of illegitimate authority, I'll get gunned down by some right-wing gun nut, who doesn't think I'm radical enough and considers me a hypocrite for voting for a candidate from one of the major parties ten years prior.

I honestly prefer this scenario to the prospect of having my family watch me suffocate on my own fluids, with bed sores and a tube in my dick. It's all pretty gross. There's nothing pretty about death, With one notable exception.

That's why I'm aiming to go out like Evelyn McHale,

Who jumped off the Empire State Building on May 1st 1947, plummeting some 1,000 feet to land on the roof of a limousine and look like she's sleeping. I'd even leave a similar suicide note, basically saying "I'd make a shitty husband and father, and you're better off without me."

But then, I'm not suicidal or depressed. I just want to go out with a smile on my face

And then be off to who knows where.

Maybe I'll visit an underwater house that's part of some weird,
aquatic purgatory,
But I don't dream about that anymore.
I still dream about my dad though.
Sometimes he's sick or dying,
But other times he's healthy
And younger,
And we solve mysteries together.
I think about these things on slow days at work, when the doors are
shut and I'm cleaning up, getting ready to go home
To my apartment,
Which I've decorated, as much as one can on a budget of zero, to
look vaguely like a set from a '30s period film.
I'll be there
By myself,
But no longer under water.

Alex Pogosov

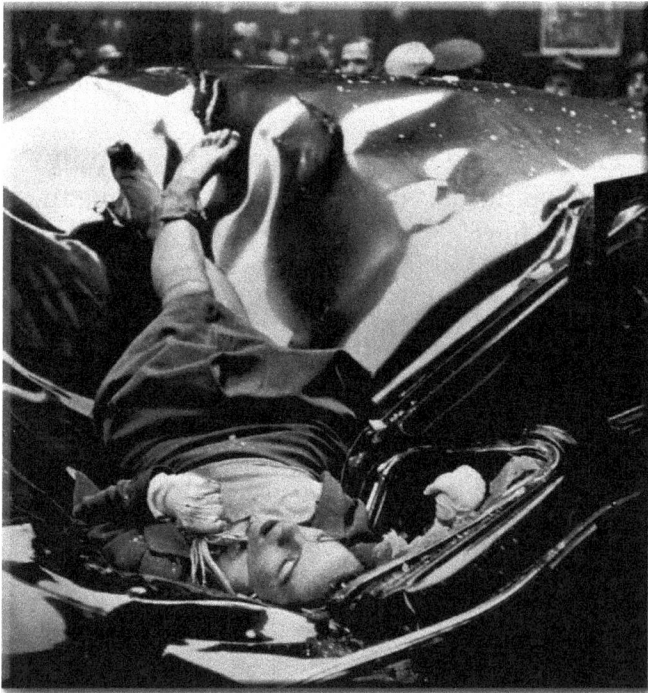

Photo of Evelyn McHale
by Robert Wiles, 1947

Broken Mends

Mom ended the conversation with
"get yourself together Christopher"
"I'm not always going to be here for you!"
As if that's not what I've been doing
These last twenty six years

I work in a shadow chrysalis industry, compensating
rusted prayers and rocking chair dreams with
witching hour transfigurations of opaque therapy
Yet I hit a wall in the cosmos of
Beautiful ugly

Stuff I've avoid for years, a memory
eviscerated from a cantankerous subconscious
that races toward success, one slow death suicidal thought
leaked from an I. V. drip, one drop
every five clicks of a stopwatch

This is wrist flick whip cracks that don't open flesh
But rip it from bone

It's the solace of bare fist, smashing
against concrete, tossing
crimson contemporary expressionist splatters
on walls

this is my master piece
a 38 year old psychologically discombobulated black man
running full speed to the edge of insanity
to exchange all second chances
for the opportunity to get it right the first time

I've heard every answer
One ever searches for
Is inside you

I have a universe of questions
where a heart should be, my veins
a jeopardy solar system, I need space
away from myself
because thinking in the Socratic method, is living
in an aggravating interpersonal communicative stardust filled
labyrinth

I can't believe I woke up one day with a room full of luggage
And nowhere to go, With
all this packed baggage, I got to go somewhere
Even if I drive myself crazy
At least then there's a reason for carrying
So much hurt and anger

it funny
how adults view their childhood
Different from their parents
Maybe it's got something to do with parents being part of the
problem
Or maybe it's got something to do with
We never really grow up
We just continuously grow

Maybe that's why at thirty eight
I find myself with a whole set
of brand new shiny situations
kept secret since twelve
I guess something's are just easier to play with
In the dark

Something's like little boys
Better seen and not heard

Because trust is ugly
And monsters aren't always mean
But you can always trust mean people
To do monstrous things to children
Yet no matter how something makes you feel
If you don't see it happening
It becomes tolerable

I read somewhere
The addict's way of handling life
Is to live in a futuristic fantasy world
Where you just wake up better
These days I'm addicted to breathing

got a knapsack of crucifixes
backpacking through lucid visions
Of tomorrows better me
Carrying so many crosses
crush exhalation from lung
making inspiration impossible

The man is just the picture on the box
Of what the boy is supposed to look like when complete
Ma, you're right
You're not going to always be here for me
But as far as getting it together Ma
There are pieces to this puzzle missing
Which keeps me undone

I may not be how you pictured me, ma
But when you have no help putting yourself together
After repeatedly being shattered
Picture perfect is not what you see on the box
But what happens when fingers get tired of puzzling

Christopher Johnson

Old Father, Old Artificer

When I was twelve I saw my father die for the first time.
He took the pill, swallowed, twenty minutes later
blank eyes opened like graves
where lotus once stood
roots plucked and frozen
in a winter of guilt, thawing upon
the return of waking life.

My father would then rise the next day,
go through the motions of working life,
arrive home, take the pill, swallow.
Lithium dreams blackened reality
like squid ink pluming
in a cloud of self-defense–
only the predator was blind,
and hunted by scent.

Father would come home to his section 8 efficiency,
look around and dislike what he saw,
then he took the pill, swallowed,
but one day it wasn't enough.
The reality of his life bloomed
like a blood orchid,
father was a murderer, twice over
father was a sexual delinquent,
father was discharged, dishonorably
father was raising twins
father was stuck and lived like a foot
in a black shoe,
and there was no "I do"
in the midst of all the gobbledygook

Father came home and wanted a way out,
he looked at the gas oven, pondered his escape
but instead took the pill, swallowed,
was cradled and rocked by a lithium carbonate
dose upped by our family practitioner.
black smoke covered hazel eyes
bright with pinpoint green
pupils like a supernova exploding
through the window of his soul.

I asked my father, "Dad are you okay?"
His breath short, he stormed out of the room
came back with a bat, pushed me up against the wall
swung the metal at my head. I ducked.
As father died, shards of plaster
splintered the air, drywall spurted
into a cloud. I slid down the wall,
my back against it for support.
And when the smoke cleared,
father was crying, lamenting his lost mind.

Ten years later, my father asked me if I'd seen it.
I just shook my head, eyes glazed from wine,
hardened to hide the hearts I'd broken,
turned my head, tipped the glass, swallowed
into shaky lights, blurred lips, and slurred breath
hands groped, hair pulled, ass smacked
living with someone inside who I did not know.
living on the edge of poetry.

Father still comes home looking for his mind,
skin sagging, veined, and cadaverous
a corpse in search of brains, it's almost comically
drenched in cliché. He doesn't find it, gives up,
takes the pill, swallows, takes another, swallows

black covers cataract eyes of faded blue
smoky hum-haze lullabies a heavy mind
dipped in silence so loud it screams–
but he cannot hear, for he is old and withered.

I watch him in his fetal-position sleep.
For a moment I think to tell him
that I have finally found his mind.
But how will I ever explain
that it is in my head?

Evan Bryant Patton

Unboxed

I held her tight
Her weight in my lap
boxed
to let her go gently
Water & wind ready to embrace her

The sun falling halfway
Our metal casket gleaming mid-flight

I needed her weight
in my lap
Not wanting to give her up
I thought I'd swallow just one bit of her
Take her in and make her stay
But she had chosen differently
Forcing me to reach into that wooden box
for her
And holding her one last time
extending my arm out into open air
fingers begrudgingly freeing
dropping her from sky
I let her go

Heather M. Browne

Death is not the Problem, Death is the Solution

At the edge of the world
sits a woman with a swaddling dress.
She's seen it all, minds destroyed
by reason and the soundest philosophies,
the unfailing war of Atlantis,
power and equality stretched
across the timeless void.

I saw the struggle in one moment
with my father in the fetal position
close to defeat, saying "I don't know,
Evan, I'm just tired of fighting."
After I told him of his son's impending death.
Eyes dried and weathered, like an aged elephant's,
his open soul flooded, but there was no fight left
for the tide to spill from his eyes.
And so I held him, my father,
like a baby.

"Don't give up on life yet,
not on living," I told this
to a man who had taken two lives,
escaped prosecution by the technicality
of a foreign country and a few shades of luck.
He lay there, in my arms,
facing the death of his blood,
like the first time a child
grasps death's meaning with his soul
and learns what it means to live.

Here in my arms, he let me feel
a father's love, when your life
is no longer your own.

As my father rose, taking back his life
I saw the fight again.
The fight of centuries
over peace, over harmony
over the timeless condition.
Then that woman leant down,
covered my face in her swaddling cloth,
and she told me her name.

Evan Bryant Patton

Scrubbing

I cleaned out my Father's closet
cupboards
drawers
Strangely touching tee shirts
Oddly packing
his green tartan boxers

90 years reduced to trash bags
bunch of books for the library
silver coin or two
photo here or there
none with me

I cleaned out my Father's life
Boxed it up
packed away
taped it closed
shut
to be dumped
trashed
tossed

I cleaned out
my Father
Dusting away his looks
washing off his words
peeling away his presence
scrubbing out
his touch

Heather M. Browne

**Opposite: "Watching Over Me"
by Claire Ibarra**

I've lived in that house.

I've lived in that house, on the edge of a cliff. Only it wasn't a house, and the cliff was time, and my mother was the wrecking ball. The cliff gave way, my mother came swinging through, and there was nothing left of the house.

I've lived in that house, only it wasn't a house, it was a trailer, it was always a trailer and it was always trailer trash men. And the tornado that roared through the chronological trailer park of our lives, she was my mother. But sometimes it would be him, whoever he may be.

I've lived in that house, only it wasn't a house it was a highways and hedges mission, and when I graduated high school, we were living with crackheads and drug fiends who were pretending they found the lord. Our mission was to get the fuck out of there, but at the time, our only other options were real highways and hedges. It was literally my mother's way or the highway.

I've lived in that house, only it wasn't a house, it was a motel room near Six Flags Over Georgia where she brought a strange man to do cocaine with while we excitedly waited to ride the rides the next day. The closest we got to real thrills that day was standing in line with momma and the man, waiting to get in and watching white stuff come out of her nose and mouth as officers surrounded us like a wildfire. The only flag she was waving that day was a white one. Cocaine white. I surrender.

I've lived in that house, only it wasn't our house, it was a crack house where she had dropped us off with a fat black lady to play with us downstairs, while she went upstairs with a big black guy to do cocaine and crack. I don't even remember what we played, I guess I was just wondering what kind of game was so fun she had to do it with someone else. And upstairs.

I've lived in that house, only it was a trailer again, as I tried to tell my mother who I really was, but was treated with disgust. I tried to tell her I was bisexual, and she blamed it on other people. I tried to tell her I was bisexual, and she said she could tell because of the way I was acting a fool in the bars when I got drunk. I tried to tell her I was bisexual, and she told me that I was not a gay baby, and she had some kind of brain scan of me that proved it.

I've lived in that house, only it wasn't a house it was a war zone. Whether it was her and dad, her and Mike, her and Thomas, her and Chance, her and Tony, her and Joe, her and Gene, her and Roy, take your pick. I've witnessed physical violence, mental torture, sexual abuse, and emotional distress so many times I can't even count all the men she let hurt us.

I've lived in that house, that foster home, two of them actually. There was the bad one and the good one. While mom was cleaning up, we were dealing with a redneck family of abusive Pentecostal idiots. The other family was nice, rich, patient, willing to teach us. It was actually one of the happiest times in my childhood. I was actually stable enough to do well in school, and I started birdwatching , and I actually played sports. They loved us more than we thought we could be loved, we even had our own version of grandparents, which we've never had before. And then mom took us back, and ripped us away from stability and sanity, and back to a life of the same abuse, minus the drugs. When I left that house, I cried harder than I thought possible. I still can't find them.

I've lived in that house, in that space with my mothers contempt for me until we were in public. In a place that made me paranoid and afraid. In a place that taught me the value of locks, and good people. In a place where mediocrity ran rampant and if you settled for less, you pretended you got what you wanted. In a place where your worst enemy could be your best friend, and then be your worst enemy again. In a place that tried to destroy my creativity, that wouldn't listen to my young poems about abuse and death, that stifled my very being unless I was being what she wanted me to be.

I've lived in that house, the one that we had to run away from, as he tried to grab the window and break it as we pulled away, as he threatened to kill us, as he tried to stop us from leaving, with me on my mother's back with two casts on my legs, which were still healing from surgery. I flailed with my mother as she punched him right in the chest, and he finally stepped away.

I've lived in that house, where the most evil of her husbands watched me shower, where he hit my mother in front of me over and over and told me to stay out of it, where he sat in the parking lot of a grocery store in his truck, lying in wait until women, some with children, would walk by the truck, and then he just started masturbating in front of them. Whatever did she see in that sicko?

I've lived in that house, where I was told I wasn't allowed to go anywhere without my mother, and that if I didn't straighten up my act she would put me in a mental institution. Where I was told she would follow me for ever and ever and I would never be rid of her. Where she controlled my SSI, my food stamps, my medication, and my entire life.

I've lived in that house, where she was trying to teach me to drive, and I didn't want to. Where she asked me to take the trash out to the dumpster at the end of the dirt road with the truck, everyday as driving practice. Where one day I was playing video games and I got angry because I was a stupid kid and didn't want to do it. Where I had an ugly sweet dog named Bullet who would always chase the truck. So when I threw the trash in the back of the truck and sped off in anger, Bullet was right behind me, until he was in front of me, until he was under me. When I stomped on the brakes and got out, horrified, he was bleeding to death and all fucked up. Mom and her stupid ass boyfriend ran out there, put Bullet in the back of the truck, chastised me, and drove me home. He didn't have a gun to put the dog down, and he wanted to teach me a lesson I'd never forget. So he drowned the dying dog slowly with the hose, and he forced me to watch as the life faded from his eyes. And mom didn't say a thing. Not until he asked me to bury the dog. Only then was it over the line. I spent six full hours crying my eyes out. And people wonder why I don't fucking drive.

I've lived in that house, on the edge of a cliff. Only it wasn't a house, and the cliff was time, and my mother was the wrecking ball.

And I was the house.

James Barrett Rodehaver

Silent Dog

The kitchen floor
is cool smooth even
patchwork squares
of lemon-lime linoleum.
Momma says key-lime
and lemon-cream.
I'm in the kitchen helping
and racing Matchbox cars.
Today is my birthday.
Our new dog barks A LOT.
The kitchen window faces west
and the late afternoon sun.
The kitchen fills
with the competing smells
of finished Kools and starting pot roast,
baking dough and brussels sprouts.
Brussels sprouts are Papa's favorite.
Supper is always at five.
Half of November is gone.
Outside the air is cold.
Through the glass the sun is warm.
The linoleum is ridged and grooved
like my knuckles or the bumps that run
in a straight line down our new dog's back.
The back of Papa's hand reminds me
to teach the new dog to sit quietly
and to remember to always do as we are told.
The sun is hot.
Half my face is on fire.
I'm glad one of my Matchbox cars is an ambulance.
Today is my birthday.
From the counter the radio announced

that a man jumped off the overpass
yesterday right after noon.
My favorite sandwich is a toasted bagel
with salmon cream cheese and whole green olives
or day old meatloaf on honey wheat.
The jumper's family mentioned that recently
he had been hearing voices and I wondered
if that jumper-man was only doing what he was told.
Momma closed her eyes and said a prayer.
Papa closed his eyes and did two shots
or maybe two shots times two more.
(When Jim Beam was talking Papa always did as he was told)
I closed my eyes and wished for a little brother or sister
and then opened them and the wish was over and no candles to blow out
but Papa there close with steely breath and scissors ready to give me a special haircut.
Monday is picture day at school.
Not much later I learned that bangs are meant to be straight
and if the camera really adds ten pounds it isn't in your hair.
Today is my birthday and I am so very excited I forgot to let out the dog.
It was then a new smell rose to compete with the other kitchen odors.
And my Papa with his fine nose for new smells like dog's waste in the family room.
Smelling it Papa grabbed a broom,
the thick and heavy kitchen broom,
and broke it like a shot over our new dog's back,
over Oscar's back,
our new dog's name is Oscar,
our Miniature Schnauzers name was Oscar,
if I hadn't mentioned it before,
and my favorite color used to be red
and whole green olives are salty and good
and meatloaf always tastes better the next day
and today is my birthday
and the broom handle broke
and its million of tiny wooden bits exploded in a cloud like tears or snow or death
if your tears were cold dead jumper-men jumping off an eyelash overpass

in the middle of a blizzard in your kitchen in November on your birthday.
And we had Papa's brussels sprouts for dinner
and between shots he said, "Paulie, it's your birthday clean up can wait—eat, eat."
And now I know that brussels sprouts taste like silent dog and coward's spit
and Matchbox cars are for little kids and barking dogs
and what do I care my hair will grow back soon anyway
because today is my birthday,
only three-hundred and sixty-five more days to go.

Paul Koniecki

being supportive

"I just can't take that woman,"
the Nursey hissed,
as she put her bra on backwards,
and reached for her drink:
"how much longer do I have
to suffer," she moaned,
as she fixed her eyes on me;

"ah, my love," I said to her,
"how much acceleration
do you need?"

"ha-ha," she said, "don't be
a madman and tempt me like that,"

and I replied that I dwell
in a state of madness,
fueled by temptation;
events only turn
by the hands of the clock:

as a younger man,
I caused such tragedies
for a tidy fee;
now, I so engage for free,
making people cry,
just to watch the tears flow,

just to watch the tears flow.

Ricky Pursley

For Andreas

My cousin is a lover.
Considers himself one of the best lovers in the world.
He loves so deeply he laughs until he cries.
He loves so deeply he cries until he laughs.
He loves so deeply he cries until he can not cry anymore.
He loves so deeply he laughs until he can not laugh anymore.

He is a survivor.
Knows his wife didn't want him to find her hanging.
She was convinced she was a burden to him,
to the three remaining children. He thinks she would
not have killed herself if little Jakob hadn't died.

He knows it's sometimes harder to live than to die.
Sometimes pain engulfs. He can't hide his grief.
Some things one never recovers from. He thinks
she would be alive if she wasn't molested as a child.

He says he will never be touched as deeply as she touched him.
He loved her the moment he saw her.
He knows she felt unworthy. She felt shame.
He thinks she would be alive if he had listened.

He's a searcher. He has always been one.
He thinks too much, and possibly too deeply.
His wife was depressed. He is depressed.
He thinks she would be alive if she took the pills.

At the funeral he said he would not love again.
Yet, my cousin a lover; one of the best lovers in the world.
Sometimes he laughs so deeply he cries.
Sometimes he cries so deeply he laughs.

Susan Dobbe Chase

Opposite: Painting by A Nero

#calamities

When the unexpected and tragic happens, it can be very difficult to make sense of life or the world. But if we are still standing when the dust settles, we have an opportunity to turn our suffering into triumph, and to show the world that we are strong enough to survive anything.

Painting by A Nero

Absolute Entity

Eyes tried to paint the view
with lashes dipped in red
on tongue
no solvent was left.

Voice knocked debris
echo didn't coerce
senses lay numb
under collapsed structure.

Life fought beleaguering death
beneath reduced world
every breath left
existence in zilch.

Amid this stillness; the tranquility
of hypothetical cipher
smothered, strangled, silenced
there laid an absolute entity.

Aparna Pathak

Firefighters.

Their faces change with love—
The kind that never dies—
And deepens by surprise
After fire, medical, wreck, flood.
Stark reality lives in their eyes.

Their start is a steady haste
Black-top and yellow lines stretched long
Become sooty foot courses
Of sofa, album, bookcase, bed
And charred relief that no one's dead.

They lift up the living
And are the first to know
Which ones have met the light
Beneath the blue, red, yellow, white
Flashing long into the night.

They move like rescue dancers,
Fluid in their husky reflective suits,
When time won't widen with hydraulic pincers—
While blood, antifreeze, oil, tears
Pool in their hearts.

Volunteer or full-time heroes
Called to act on enduring duty;
As preparation becomes real caring—
For patient, victim, friend, neighbor
Fallen, and unable to rise alone.

Terri Richardson

The Last Time That The World Ended

The last time that the world ended, I was there
 We rushed in like Angels
  They let me be an angel, the last time that the world ended.

It was the worst storm,
The strongest twister,
The biggest fire,
The most noble war.
And we tried, we tried...
 to pull innocence from the twisted rubble,
 we brought people off of roofs.
  there were army rations and Red Cross cots
  and visits from Presidents and Governors

We searched house to house,
  removed fallen trees from post-storm streets
    spray painted X's on front doors as each home was cleared
No expense was spared, the last time that the world ended

 New Orleans, Texas, New York City
Alabama, Mississippi, New Orleans again

Disaster becomes only a word after too long
And grief always looks the same from the sky

When every storm is the worst storm

How many times have I rebuilt my life?
How much destroyed or left behind,

by forces of nature, by acts of God, by mindlessness and
happenstance?
Where were the legions of angels, then?

So, this time, I will not run into the disaster,
 the stars do not call to me personally anymore, for they have been
told to be wary of my weariness
   I am no longer on the roster of super heroes, now that my own
disasters have been shared.
I will not look into loss-filled eyes this time.
I will not know the stench of human decay in sun-drenched
suburbs.
There will be no reassurances, no comforting, no glorious god-less
faith in man...

How close is too close to stand,
 The next time the world decides to end?

PW Covington

Twisting and Turning

They came so fast
With my eyes to the sky
And my ear to the news
I wanted to cry.

So many tornadoes playing tag in Indiana and Kentucky
Too many to count
Our newscasters couldn't keep up.
"Be prepared to take cover. We don't know where they will strike,"
 Was all they could say.

Have you ever known that deep fear that strikes at your core
An unknown danger that could sweep your entire life away?
Hours upon hours, I waited for my fate.

Reports poured in of the tornadoes' destructive game.
Up and down the Ohio River they raced.
Teasing me with their power
Taunting me with their destruction.

The alarm sounded so fast.
Quick! Take cover!
The EF-4 tornado that destroyed Henryville, Indiana is heading
straight for Carrollton, Kentucky!
Carrollton, take cover! Take cover now!
The newscasters warn as the alarm blasted its sirens.

Grab the pets.
Wake my husband up.
Run to the basement.
Oh, God I can hear my roof shaking!

"Facing the Storm" by Maranda Russell

I crouch next to my husband
Our hands entwined and our prayers lifting high in the air.
Oh, God, hear our pleas.
I'm not ready to die.

The roof shakes.
What was I thinking living in a three story Victorian home?
Tumble, grumble.
It passes overhead.
Don't land on me! Don't land on me!
Oh, God, don't land on me!

Minutes pass like hours.
My heart races with every beating second.
The alarm dies down.
I'm still alive.
The tornado has left the area.
Thank God. I'm alive.

Out of the depths I climb to see the destruction.
That fateful event left unseen scars.
Three times the tornado landed.
Carrollton should have been wiped off the map.

Lives and property destroyed.
The monster seeks to take it all.
Henryville, Indiana
New Liberty, Kentucky
Only a few names I will never forget.

Grateful and yet humble
I will never forget my date with the monster in the air.
Residents from all over Kentucky and Indiana helped one
another in a way I had never seen before.

Separated by a large river but united by our hearts.

There's power in a community that stands together after a disaster. It's amazing to see how a diverse group of people from all over the region can bond and help one another through the toughest of days. Moore, Oklahoma will survive, too.
They shall overcome.

Allison Bruning

"Ours is not to wonder why..."

I met him in a cattle trailer, redesigned to transport soldiers.
We, being young, and cruel beyond our comprehension,
found it hilarious that the fat kid was riding with us.
Asking, "Do you feel at home?"
We all knew, he would have a hard time, that he would make it harder on all of us.
We hoped he would fail, early on, save us from extra effort.
He hung tough, even though his weight and size slowed us down.
The thought never crossed our minds, that he, knowing it would be extra difficult
volunteered anyway. He had to know it would be harder for him, more than anyone.
It was.
The Drill Sgt.'s didn't disappoint, Pvt. Fat Boy, and others were his name, for weeks.
When inspection came one day, and the candy bars were found,
I being his squad leader and he being caught with caloric contraband,
were road marched out into the darkness of the Georgia pine forest.
I, stood at attention while the newly crowned Pvt. Candy Bar dug a foxhole to army specs:
Two helmets wide, two M-16's long, and armpit deep.
The last resting place of his shame, and betrayal to his squad.
There was no sleep that night, for either of us.

The whole squad suffered for his weakness the next day,
and at the end of it, in the showers, we beat the crap out of him,
naked, vulnerable, and now crying, his debt to us was paid,
the evidence of his blood washed down the drain with his weakness.
We were ordered not to let him fail, the brotherhood we had joined, "Leaves no man behind"
we pulled him back up, and we all succeeded. We graduated Basic,

then went off to our duty stations, I never saw him again.

Until his Wife, found me on Facebook.

Private Candy Bar went on to do a 2 year tour in Korea, a year in Germany, 3 in Iraq, and two in Afghanistan.

She contacted me to inform me of his death.

She said he fell from a blackhawk, in a training exercise, that his safety belt wasn't fastened correctly. She tells me about how he's been quiet, seeking seclusion a lot, and how he was gaining back his weight. She said,"I thought it might have been a suicide."

After the funeral, when the bank called to tell her about a safety deposit box,

she went to clean it out, she knew then, her guess was right.

Next to a 9mm pistol, was the NOTE, picture of us at graduation and Crown Royal bag.

The bag contained finger bones and foreskins, of his enemies.

The pistol had one round in it.

The note simply read, "You should have let me fail."

Stephen Lawson

Connect the Wild Dots

"poems from the edge of help"
for Mark J Kilroy

Sara came from Texas.
I crossed over for Spring Break.

The circus has a juggler.
The border has a war.

The street has a taco vendor,
two lamp posts, and a trick.

The air is hot and sweet.
Breathing is a pilgrimage.

I need a bag.
Breathing is inalienable.

I need a bag.
The hoarders have a brick.

Obliterated on cerveza fria
we cross the street to get a bag.

The streetlight slits the darkness
like a razor on the bias.

In the shadows
brick stacking hoarders pause to ask my name.

Adrenaline is a blessing.
Breathing is circus work.

Breathing is an artifice, a subterfuge,
an almost involuntary trick.

The circus has a jugular.
The border has a war.

El Padrino has a farm outside of town.
Matamoras has a witch.

Dirt cannot be shoveled
by the sleeping and the dead.

I need a bag. I need a bag.
I need a bag.

Sara came from Texas.
La Madrina is six foot one.

The names have not been changed
because the innocent are dead.

I looked for God twelve times.
Twelve times in a hole I looked.

I love you the perfectness of death.
Her lips are soft on soft.

Beyond torture. Beyond pain.
Beyond clean blood and the integrity of maggots.

Twelve times in the hole spooning dirt and worms
and the ends of lost mistaken things and machetes in the neck.

Little tarot boy of Mexico City

thank you for not burying me alone.

Pain is a beginning.
The border's war is drugs.

I need a bag. I need a bag.
I need a bag of air.

Paul Koniecki

Short Final
(Somalia 1992-93)

How old were you in 1992?
I was 18, and I was not an infantryman
Yet at Christmas time I flew to war
On Comet, on Cupid, on Donner, and Blitzed in
...into Mogadishu on a Hercules
I was not an infantryman
News cameras and equatorial black faces swarmed us at the airport
Chanting, USA! USA!
At night, mortars would fall
Shaking the ruined walls we reclined behind,
Death, daring us to sleep
Always the shit-smell of the air
Would hang visible on short final
Short final—about to hit ground
In 1992 I was 18
And I was not an infantryman
That place couldn't keep up with all the death I saw
Bodies would lay atop each other in the streets,
Along with camels and dogs,
And brass shell casings and spent RPG tubes
It would percolate and boil and bake and steam,
And sometimes explode
We'd scramble for cover
I was not an infantryman
I was not an infantryman,
Any killing that I did
Came later
In a bottle,
In a letter,

In a whorehouse,
In a thousand ways,
Thousands of miles away
After friend and foe,
lover and stranger,
right and wrong and Jesus Christ
Just didn't matter anymore.
I was not an infantryman
I didn't get to fire back
When sniper fire would shatter the ramp concrete into powder at
our heels
As we worked to offload the tools of conflict
Or upload the injured and the dead...the only spoils of war I ever
saw, but...
I was not an infantryman
That little war of my youth
gets lost, over looked
Between the faded flag confetti of so called desert Victory
And this current sticky mire
I'm left to soldier on
But I am not an infantryman
And short, short final
Can last for decades
Like a free-fall of free-floating detachment
Still airborne
Still hanging somewhere over East Africa
A mist of useless, irrelevant, dismissed regret
Just a few colored ribbons to my name
I have nothing heroic to tell you about
I was not an infantryman

PW Covington

You Take From Me

Author's Note: You Take From Me was written for a therapist friend whose father went through the Holocaust. She is Jewish. Her parents and siblings were eventually reunited praise God, but everything beyond family, faith and love was gone. They felt fortunate. Both her parents died many years ago. She recently received a notice for her Dad that the German government was demanding reimbursement funds as they claimed they had given him too much. She was outraged and reached out. This was my gift to her:

You take from me
my home
my job
my wife
my kids
This is war you say
But you do not ask of me
You take from me my
freedom
voice
purpose
This is war you say
And never ask of me
You take
my land
my safety
dreams
It's just the way it is in war you know
Yet never ask of me
And when Your war is finally through
and now my internal war has start...
This was only war you say
And never ask of me
Out I'm tossed
No need to hold

No need to keep
There's nothing left
no home
no place
no one
not one
a few dollars you toss
Really only war you know
And still... you never ask of me
So many years have come and gone
My second life as well
And yet you say
of what we took
your home
your job
your life
your wife
your kids
freedom
voice
all these things
all this all
we gave too much
so much
so much
those dollars tossed
so many
too many for your loss
You take from me
once more
Seventy years later more
Although I'm not here for you to take
you take once more
and never ask of

Heather M. Browne

Static

The hum of the cars outside your window
the alarms, the sirens, the screams, the gunshots.

For the first couple weeks you awake to the slightest creek or tap outside.

You run to the window. You peer outside. See what's going on.

You are aware of everything.

You are awoken by the sound of laughter on the first night. So you went to the front door and looked into the courtyard where you saw 3 naked women jumping in the pool.

That's a nice welcome home sight to see.

Children across the street playing in the yard. They nearly run into the street and your heart panics for them as you fear they'll be hit by a speeding car.

The dogs down the way running all over the place. Amazing none of them have been hit yet.

The mad pedestrians waiting at the bus stop just a few yards away. Some of them speak to themselves and fight with the invisible man. Then they get on the bus and shut up and act like normal citizens.

Like nothing was ever wrong.
Maybe it wasn't.

You sitting, silently observing and judging, analyzing, meditating.

Tracing down all the details in your mind. These are things that get your attention. These are the elements of your life in this moment.

A large naked black woman is found drown in the pool 3 weeks after you move in.

No one knows who she is or where she came from.

Strange.

Everything is muted now.

Ivy on the walls,
Children in the pool.
Crazy ass neighbors pounding the walls with bass beats at 4 in the morning.
Sirens wailing at all hours.

Nothing new.

listening to the 300lb stomper upstairs who carries the weight of the world on her shoulders and masks it with a 110lb body and a muted face.

It bothers you that you'll never know why she is always so angry or what she does for a living. But it's ironic because you do not really want to know because it would ruin the image of her. It would erase the character you've aptly nicknamed Thunder Foot.

Little yapper dogs,
alcoholics,
comedians,
a shoe designer,
a fellow writer who pounded on his typewriter every night from midnight til.......

You never even learned his name. Again, you didn't want to for fear of invading on his privacy.

The wino, the liar, the cheat, the slut, the cougar, the one who needs to know the details of everyones life but rarely speaks of her own. The one who never works.

The swingers living upstairs with their kids and mom.

Dexter, the cat.

Sammy the dog

Richie the black shaggy dog.

Interesting people. A menagerie of character flaws to study.

These were your neighbors.

You became so accustomed to these new surroundings that you forgot to take note of them. It all became static. Ambiance in the background of your life. Just another noise.. no big deal..

It's quiet now. Everyone is gone. All that remains is You. and 8 other residents. Now that the static is gone you can hear the birds again. The sirens outside the window are alarming once again.

You're taking notice.
Actively recording the elements of the past year.

Never let life become ambient.
You must remain actively observant to everything.

Don't allow yourself to be desensitized to day to day living.

After all that's where the magic moments are hidden.

Nothing is trivial.
Nothing is static.

Are you paying attention now?

WC Chambers

Painting by A Nero

#lovegonewrong

Many times love, or the loss of it, can be the greatest source of pain of all. For many, it is difficult to cope once they have been betrayed, abused, or neglected by the one person charged with loving them unconditionally, and treating them right. But if we can survive someone else's cruelty and the pain of utter heartbreak we are left with when they are gone, we can find out for ourselves that the greatest love of all must be self love. We must love ourselves first and know that we are enough, that we are loved by those around us who know how to love us, and that we can survive the aftermath of a love gone wrong.

Exposed

Those forests can be only walked naked,
on the soft, at parts bebarked paws
of the once-tamed-but-escaped,
of the fairly-wild-still.

I shush along the trees you sculpted for me,
embarrassed by your shiny touch
on the leaves which unfold
curved trajectories to the Deepest.

The Dreamiest Alone has never scared me.
I keep talking to you as if you were
still whiskassing me until I purred.

Watching me, bastard, huh? Don't you ever stop
feasting your eyes? And what's next?
You make me jump through
mirrored sunset-flames on lakes
and when exhausted you stroke me
while I fall asleep?

I square up to you, looking straight back
to your fucking fingers,
I can bite and hiss until you
keep out of my sight.
Pardon my French, I'm supposed to speak like a lady
but it's gone, I've unalterably changed.

Vulnerable at core but keep going.
The more I scream, the more silence I gain.
The more I swear at you, I become the more sacred.
You made me Goddess of Survival.

Agnes Marton

**Opposite: "Sanguine Slavery"
by TM Rhyno**

Our Penny

I get a letter every month in the mail.
Addressed to you and me.
It's from the bank.
Telling me we own one penny between us
in our joint account.
You've been gone almost 3 years now.
No interest, sad to say.
And I know I should call them,
 remind them that you're gone.
For some reason they didn't hear me when I called.
Or sent the proof.

I know I should save the trees in the forest.
The horse hooves from glue.
BofA from postal bankruptcy.
And Chuck, our mailman, the steps.
But for some reason,
I like seeing your name there in print.
Even if for just one penny.
I know you're gone,
but for that little moment
the rest of the world didn't hear
when I called.

Heather M. Browne

On Instinct:
Found Love notes

VII.

Your mouth burns,
devil caught between split tongue and charred teeth,
saliva brings a corpse to life, hopeful,
syringes rat-a-tat-tat on your forearms.

Flesh drags itself across filthy carpet,
rug burns to thighs, knees
bone cracks, haunting windows
haunting your voice.

Your voice leaves me lonely,
heavy,
juiced,
raw,
lucid.

Lucid, you leave me patiently waiting,
skin smoldering,
flirting with one broken rib—
one ripped dress—
one busted lip—
a new sort of god that forgot we were waiting.

Jennifer E. Hudgens

"C'est la vie" by Claire Ibarra

Attempted Murder of a Love Life

I want to bang my head against a wall,
that's all.
Not too much to ask:
a simple task for the simple-minded,
undecided,
people of the populace,
who feel lost from us...
because they thrust us away from them.
The last we saw,
it was all over.
Undercover lovers,
recover from the discovery of their tryst.
I mope listlessly.
Trussed by being trusting.
Whipped masochistically...
into a twisted,
sadistic,
flip of fate.
I can't wait to untouch you.
But simply,
slowly,
make see...
saw.
Operating remotely;
an emotionally repressed robot.
Time tends to trust wearingly.
Tearing me quasi-orgasmicly.
Truly only killing me,
with every sever.
Yet you continue to weather me,
with licorice-thin lips.
Hour after hour,

you become more sour than I can swallow.
Shot for shot in a sitting,
twittering in your ear.
I hate that sneer.
A queer kind of smile...
twitching,
but all the while,
still becoming.
Your laugh,
harsh and deep,
eyes up and away.
Take your words from me.
Take your physicality.
Pretend to prepare me,
for some sort of bitter agony...
as winter approaches,
and all new things,
encroach upon the old.
I'm again on the rebound.
My poetry harking aloud,
with hollow sound,
and no control over the change in beat.
It's taking a backseat to my own hands,
and I can't reprimand them.
My brain leaking onto the board that I'm
tapping.
What happened to my grasp on the reigns?
I'm racing barrels unseated,
and clenching for fear of heavy hoof to hat.
This corral has no fences,
no walls,
no constraints at all!
And I can only clench,
tense,
too scared to let go...
and fly.

Yocelin Watts

Spiraling

I don't know if I should build relationships...
...or walls.
Get my hands dirty with emotions...
...or mortar.

Life.
Spiraling.
Silent abyss.
Ineffective.
I'm drowning here.
No longer hear hope on horizon.
Hear nothing.
Atmosphere sucked away all sound.
All light.
All feeling.
Hands stretched out to me
Always out of reach.
Cries of my angels.
(Oh my God)
Cackling of demons.
This darkness...my own.

Created by insecurities.
Formed of my failures.
Not to be written in love poems
Not to be sung in songs.
This darkness, so thick,
Not quite floating...
Not quite falling...
But I... I stopped being human a LONG time ago.

Are we supposed to become this impervious to pain?

This used to sorrow?
This acquainted with agony?

Apathy... safety feature or design flaw?
Suicides... factory recalls.
Hell... chop shop where God... fixes... His... mistakes.

God,
(dammit!)
Forgive borderline blasphemy
You gotta believe I love You
And would never put anyone above You.
I can't thank You enough for all You've been to me
But something's got to give!
Does my Christian Express Card
Have a high enough limit
To buy another catalyst for praise
Cause I stopped cheating on You a long time ago but
The interest rates on these loyalty tests are KILLING me.

I'm dying here!

Love. (huh!)
Norris said love is choosing the biggest lie
You were willing to believe in
And I believed in them all.
All I've ever wanted...to be loved
Honestly.
Completely.
My willingness to bend appreciated.
My love looked for diligently and found.
Someone to love me like I love me
Cause I've even learned how to masturbate my own emotions.
I believed in love like some people believe in fairy tales.

But
this
hurts.

Oh, God, this hurts.

This hurt,
This darkness,
Filling my lung's capacity,
So angry, so complete,
Such violence, such deceit.
Can't tell the difference between it
And Your light that inhabits me.
This dichotomy taunts me.
Fear... faith... laughing at me
I wanna scream
But it's taken even that away from me

I'm suffocating here!

Somebody help me.

My hands... are getting dirty here.

Somebody... trust me.

Your lies... are blinding me.

Somebody guide me.

I'm lost here.

Somebody... find me.

Tavis P. Brunson

Abuse

I had not considered the word before—
     it slipped from my father's mouth
     with ease, the night
     he made you leave
it hung, suspended
in a space where I could not yet grasp
it. Hours later, when the house was silent
     the bedroom spotless
     sheets changed, furniture moved
to disguise the scenery
Google informed me via a list of yes or no
questions   —does he, do you—
that the word suspended
midway between the kitchen slate
and the popcorned ceiling was the name
     of seven years.

Sharon Sitler

Simple Confession

There was a young poet
thin, emerging from
his chrysalis of drugs
Christ-like,
surrounded by blue fire.
I was a young girl
learning the names
of molecules, bird, and songs.
He was 17, I was 15.
I was the last person
That spoke to him
before his overdose.
I fell asleep clinging
to the telephone.
I knew I loved him
but I never imagined
that 13 years later
I'd marry him.
I would have one
son while he was imprisoned.
Then we would have twins.
He fucked my best friend
before we left Houston
and moved north to grow grapes
and make wine.
We lived by a beautiful lake
and played in the sun—
we made love every day—
but his demons never went away.
He tried to kill me twice.
I loved him so much
I might have let him

take my life—
but there were these
amazing children we had
spawned in our maelstrom
of creation, not of our imagination.
There was no turning back.
I told him not to make me choose.
But he did.
The police came after I ran into
the street screaming.
There was no hiding
the cuts on my face.
It was over.
The cops took him away.
They told me I'd lose my children
if I stayed.
He was free the next day.
I divorced him.
I moved to Dallas to get as
far away as the courts
would let me go,
a protective order in
my glove compartment,
sleeping with only one eye closed.
I sent hundreds of his poems
back, carefully sealed in
Ziploc bags because I knew
he wouldn't take care of them—
but I didn't want them either.
Now I see him every other
weekend when we exchange
the kids for visitation.
He still wants to talk about
poetry and sex.
I still write. He doesn't.

He texted me the lyrics to
The Electrician—a song
about torturing someone
with electricity.
He says it's poetry.
I'm not sure what message
was meant for me.
My shrink diagnosed me
with depression and PTSD.
All I want is protection.
I look at my reflection
and wonder who I used to be.
Will he murder me
quietly with dread?
How long will his poems
ring in my head?
I love him and
I wish he was dead.

Trier Ward

#scars

Whether physical, mental, or emotional, the scars we acquire from living hard lives can be painful reminders of what we endured, or proud emblems of a life well lived. But if we can overcome what made those scars, we can overcome any that might be made in the future. Our scars tell our story, and no matter how many we wind up having, or how we feel about them, in the end, they are testaments to our powerful will to survive.

a letter to me from my scar

I was born from smooth flesh.
Mother was a wound.
Father was the time it took for the blood to clot.
Stitches embraced me,
good friends.
They held me, pulled me together and didn't let go
until I could do it myself,
hold myself closed,
pursed in a permanent kiss.
When they were removed
I thought I might burst.
I was tight,
raw,
scary
before the dried gore flaked away.
Born from wound and time
I am a scar,
tough tissue.
I regret that I shame you,
that you hide me.
Just like you—
it wasn't my choice to be here
and I don't want to be ugly.
Scars,
we try to be small,
we try to shrink,
fade into the surrounding flesh.
You understand that feeling.
The one on your chin,
the result of a childhood collision with pavement,
I wish I was tiny like that one,
not such an extensive roadmap to your past injury.

Opposite: "Heart Energy"
by Maranda Russell

I am a big scar,
often jealous of the love you bear
for the marks needled into your skin,
your tattoos,
your chosen scars.
I was not chosen. I was fate,
but I am so much more—
more than the terrible flaw you fear to show a future lover.
I am the thickest, strongest part of you.
I am the signature of your powerful love.
I was the curtain that parted
when your beautiful child stepped upon the stage.
Please—
when you touch the length of me,
think of her
and love me.
Understand what I represent.
Just like you
I am proof that sometimes
there is a price,
life goes on,
damage heals.
I am the strongest skin you've got.

D. Victory

Far Away.

He drinks his beer alone at night, runs through jungles in his dreams
And as he's turning out the light, he's in Saigon in '73
Came back home to lose his friends, his family, and then his wife
Now he lives in another time and they all say he's lost his mind
Calls old friends but they've moved on, a soldier's life has passed him by
Cleans his guns and lives in fear, a purple heart and wounded pride
He's gonna live until he dies in this prison he has made
His body's there in Wilsonville, but his mind is far away

She makes her bed in Tennessee and cries herself to sleep each night
Sees a young boy in her dreams, he has my nose, he has her eyes
We all told her she was wrong, she don't belong here anymore
She couldn't feed him at the time but now it's life she can't afford
Calls old friends that don't have time or want to listen as she talks
Some mistakes can't be undone and now she stares at empty walls
A little baby's precious life wasn't all she threw away
She threw away a heart and soul and I thank God she's far away

We all would take it all away if we could turn back time somehow
He broke my heart that April day but knows he's not the same man now
Can't forget what he has done, but knows he cannot change the past
So he'd forget his only son, who hoped each day would be his last
There were no friends for me to call, each day was hard just living life
He'd look at me and see her face, my mother and his former wife
No man can judge another man, we all have demons we must face
So we just take it day by day cause Heaven ain't too far away.

Eric Blackerby

Sweet Waltz.

Call me Virgin Mary, teach me how to be new
Years of side stepping, awkward fumble
I've found a pitcher filled with enough,
my bone is enough,
Body is enough,

I don't drown in your soft smiles, anymore
You found me, returned to a place I bathe in
holy water,
Sewn my paper doll limbs back together,
as though you'd never torn through them,
never should've called me baby,
or cradled me a quiet Osiris,

My spirit more oracle, sacred
Not some cavern you can covet, or stagnate in
You are rotting on your own,
Keep your trigger fingers scratched,
all ten of them,

Close your mouth, it's only catching flies and breeding maggots.

Jennifer E. Hudgens

battleground.

this is supposed to be yet another poem to quell the pain,
to turn it into glory,
to make it make sense,
to rise above it,
to be inspirational by being happy despite it,
but not today.
today, i'm a soldier in a battle whose only silver lining is seen once it's over.
there is no philosophy or clarity to be had in the middle of the battle,
there is only pain, and the need to fight,
and the desire to stay alive to see that silver lining again.
there is no wit, there is no humor, and there is very little wisdom.
there is only pain, and the only wisdom is surviving it.
there is screaming and curses to god,
and struggles to make it to the bathroom that destroy your independence and dignity.
if you want to see my bravery, come back when i'm healing, and i'll show you my scars.
right now, all i have to show you are open wounds and a faith that,
no matter how many times i rebuild it in the interim, is always shattered again.
you don't want to see the things a soldier goes through,
or has to do in order to come back home.
so write me as much as you want, and wait for me to return to myself.
and always expect to say goodbye one more time.
because i'll always be dragged back, and i'll always get wounded again,
and just in case this time is my last battle, and your last goodbye,
i'll always remember you as the silver lining i could never see until the smoke cleared,
and the pain faded.
thanks for being the reason i will always come back home.

James Barrett Rodehaver

Breast monologue

My right breast is jealous.
It's jealous of all the other breasts out there
who have a partner.
My breast is singular,
a solitary nomad wandering the earth
looking for someone to hang with.
It's jealous of all the other breasts out there
who can carry on a dialogue with each other
'cause my breast can only talk to itself,
it can only carry on a monologue like a one-woman play.
My right breast is the star of the show!
You'd think that'd make her happy
'cause sometimes
I like being the center of attention
but this kind of attention
is like being a troupe member of a freak show.
Every day my right breast sits atop my torso
like a solitary mountain at the edge of a valley.
A scar is her companion,
a red patchy scar gradually fading away
over a heart that's freezing to death, no blanket to cover it.
The companion of my breast is a sinkhole you drive your car over and get stuck in
'cause you weren't expecting it.
My prosthesis gives a convincing illusion.
The companion of my breast is a hollowed-out valley.
A green, grassy hill used to be there
but they came along and bulldozed it
'cause they found out a dragon lived inside it.
So they hollowed it out
like a cantaloupe or a honeydew melon
when you take one of those melon scoopers and scoop out the innards
to put chicken salad inside it for a delicious dish

or when you scrape out the contents of a baked potato,
prepare them with barbecued chicken, cheddar cheese, sour cream, and butter
and put them back in for another delicious dish.
But they didn't put this hill back together once they slew the dragon with the
mastectomy scalpel.
No. They left a hollowed-out valley
'cause either they didn't care
or they thought a valley would make a nice contrast sitting next to a mountain.
But the thing with mountains is, most times they're hard to climb,
they look ominous and menacing, all granite and rocky,
cold-looking the color of steel,
so people are scared of them, scared to try and climb them,
afraid they'll fall, lose their life trying.
My right breast is lonely.
She has no one to talk to but herself.
She tells herself, "I'm ugly."
She hears her defeated, sad monologue all day
while she looks down on a scar-covered valley.
The scar, looking like a bridge that goes on forever
but she knows it's a bridge to nowhere.
Every day my right breast sees me cover up this scar with a beige prosthesis
but she knows it's not real. It's not real, live flesh.
It's not a real, live breast like she is
so she knows it can't talk.
It's just a dummy, stuffed inside a white bra
like a high school girl's half-dozen Kleenex.
But at night the illusion ends as I, the ventriloquist,
take off the white bra with the dummy inside it and bare my right breast.
As I set her free, she doesn't let out a victorious cry like
"Liberty!"
She just cries
'cause she's lonely.

Lori Lasseter Hamilton

Scar-light.

We counted scars,
your stab wound,
my nervous breakdown,
letters carved into my left wrist,
used to say let go,
faded once I learned forgiveness,
your neck, my stomach
tattoos, poems in skin,
our confetti hearts still nervous,
shaken snow globes,
my ankle, your father
you looked deep into my eyes and found me,
found me beautiful,
you are beautiful,
we are a mess of beauty.

Hold my hand, it's still shaking.

Jennifer E. Hudgens

Deaf Couple

Their world a vacuum of gestures
Their language a mysterious dance
Of lips and limbs
Fingers and forms

He moves she responds
And shapes her reply
Wordless he takes it
And remodels his answer

Working their conversation
Perfecting in a soundless world
They listen without hearing
Translating the silence into meaning...

Emma van Woerkom

Scars

On my left wrist, a sideways "J"
At age four, I moved a piece of sheet metal
off my porch so I could play with my friend.
The razor-sharp corner
cut into my small wrist
missing the vein by only millimeters.

Years later, as I walked home from school
with a boy from the block
He threw rocks and one hit my forehead
I don't remember if he meant to
I've told the story so many ways
I kept walking home
The blood trickled down my face
saturating my Mickey Mouse sweater.
I had stitches
and the injury is now concealed.

The next year
I swung on the jungle gym during recess.
The bell rang and I did a flip off the bars
A screw caught my arm
Tore from inner elbow to wrist
It didn't hurt, I distinctly remember
I left school early
Got a tetanus shot
It was a big, ugly mark
that disappears more every day.

Scars—visible weaknesses—
tell tales for some
and disappoint others
I don't scar easily anymore.

Lilly Penhall

Any good.

I slide my knee-high boots on like I'm dressing for a salesman,
selling vacuums door-to-door,
seducing twenty something daughters,
longing to know what open road tastes like,
they try to find crumbs between his teeth,

stretch my arms up, admiring the weight of gravity,
laugh lines, sweet cursive on plump cheeks,
baby face hides years, hides the stranger I'm not anymore,
relish in scars near ribs, scars on palms,
hair discombobulated, wrestled my crocodile fingers

I used to think this body wasn't any good,
laugh was too loud, voice was too nasal,
singsong melody was more scratched record than beautiful,
used to think this body was deserving of dislocated ribs,
of lovers that always lie, or cheat.

I am not selling, not sold.
Not sex, not broken.
Not sex, not open for fucking.
Not sex, not waiting for white knight.

I am not a thing, not taken.
Not girl, not doll.
Not girl, not event horizon.
Not girl, not fix her.

I am woman, beautiful.
Beautiful, thunder clapped sky.
Beautiful, luminescent.
Beautiful, simply
Beautiful.

Jennifer E. Hudgens

Welcome to the show

I am a ventriloquist.
Every day, I make a dummy do what I want it to.
I stuff it inside my bra and fool you,
make you believe I have two breasts.
I am a magician, an illusionist, because really
I'm caved in on one side
like a house after a tornado
or a wall someone punched their fist through.
I strap on my prosthesis tucked away inside my bra
like someone wearing a dildo in their boxer briefs.
I mean, how enticing could I be with just one breast?
If you had to look at a flat wall
and then a bulging stomach right underneath,
could you stand it?
I know I can't.
Sometimes I can see my heart beat through my chest wall.
It's creepy
like when they show a surgical procedure on TV.
Beneath my scar, I can see a faint rising and falling back,
rising and falling back.
Boom boom,
boom boom
like a caged animal beating his cell bars trying to get out
but it's guarded, guarded by the ringmaster
wearing a bright tuxedo jacket with tails and top hat
smiling at the audience
until the lion tamer comes along and opens the cage,
cracks a whip to keep the lion in his place.
My heart is kept in place
by a white bra and a prosthesis pocketed inside it
like a handkerchief tucked inside the ringmaster's tuxedo jacket.
I carry a dummy inside my shirt daily

Opposite: Photo by Rosie Lindsey

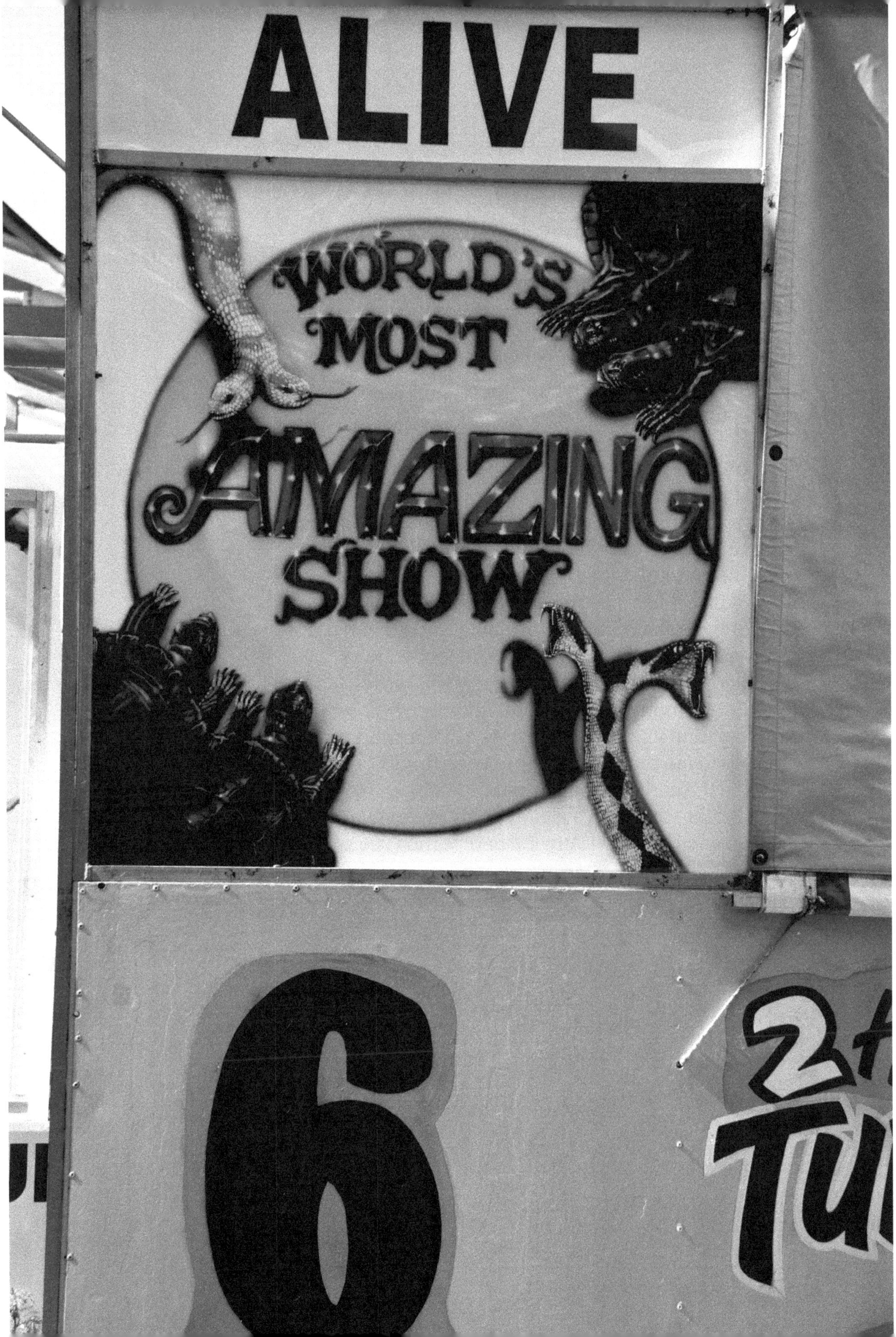
ALIVE
WORLD'S MOST
AMAZING
SHOW
6

but I don't pretend that it can talk.
You see, it can tell lies all on its own
without me moving my mouth or sticking my hand inside it to turn its head.
All I have to do is stuff it inside my shirt and it screams from its cotton coffin,
"I'm real! I'm real!"
It idolizes Pinocchio.
It wants to become dust that God spits on and turns into mud
then fashions into clay to mold a real breast
but when God put me to sleep,
He took the real breast away.
Like Job, I guess I should say "The Lord gave, and the Lord has taken away;
blessed be the name of the Lord."
I'll try to tell my dummy that, tell it to be grateful in all things
and not want so much to become real,
to just be grateful to be what it is,
grateful that it has a cotton bed to lie down in,
grateful that it has a job to do, a magic act to perform—
to stay strapped across my chest and fool you.
But I'm afraid of the repercussions it will bring.
If I tell my dummy to be grateful I know it will scream,
want to pound its claws against its cell bars and roar
so it's up to me the ringmaster to keep things quiet
and keep the audience entranced
with a bright smile and a gleam in my eye and an exuberant cry:
"Welcome to the show! Anyone here wanna see some magic tricks tonight?"

Lori Lasseter Hamilton

a million kisses and a comet's tail to the edge of the milky way

houses sleep upright
a figure eight falls on its side forever
backyard trampolines catch cold in the freezing rain
they leave me off at grandma's driveway
a toilet plunger stands in a field of many plungers
furiously waving its non-existent hands
i knock
the door opens like rivers flow or lava
flakes of cold cold snow hit the warm warm windowpane
grandma opens her mouth
i think of tympani drums or cauldrons
the egg in my pocket keeps my silly putty fresh
i am not seven
there is no circus in the snow
ice grows down
mailboxes yawn
silly putty transfers faces
grandma boils her false teeth she calls dentures
the oven's click and the stove top's orange glow
the mirror tells when she was young and beautiful and smiles
grandma chases me with her panful of still boiling false teeth water
hiss-pering something—the devil is coming the devil is coming—
i am unwilling or unable to quite hear
the universe turns and she calls me poonchka and she calls me dupa
grandma NEEDS to burn me
there must be no way out of love
i croak back i think the devil is already here

she laughs and the moment for burning is gone
passers-by break sidewalk salt under their bootheels
a shoemaker cuts his finger and works the blood in to the sole
kissing me on the neck and then again right below the ear
grandma bathes me wearing nothing but an empty toilet paper tube
grandma sings slim whitman's ooma palola blanca
ooma palola blanca i'm just a bird in the sky
ooma palola blanca over the mountains i fly
nothing can take this feeling away
my grandmother is very beautiful
burns blister blisters heal
we like people for their favors and love them for their faults
somewhere far-off i hear an accordion and the sound of people dancing

Paul Koniecki

Troubles

Watch the daylight glow.
Soak in the Light.

Listen to the voices on the wind
close your eyes and all shall be forgotten.

Troubles slumber beneath trees these days.
Troubles have lost their fear of man.

They sit and smirk while gnashing teeth in anticipation for man to
step into their strategically placed traps.
They know us to be reckless.

They can see our beauty and seek to destroy us.
Troubles are the eaters of dreams and prayers.

Be mindful of the shadows.
Keep an eye on the horizon and never look back.

Go for the long haul.
Push more than ever.

Don't be scared to sleep.
We must stay strong and alert.
Troubles feed upon the weak.

The strong will always shake them off.

Be warned my dreaming children for Troubles do exist.
They do kill the innocent and they maim the by standers who are
fearful.

Never succumb.
Never let yourself go numb.

Hold true.
Hold tight.

Live for you and that which you love the most.

Keep strangers in sight.
Keep your friends in your heart.
Love your lovers with all your heart.
Love terrifies Troubles more than anything.

Don't be scared to love all you know and do.

When doing something you hate.
Pretend to love it or it will be the thing that destroys your drive,
your ambition and your desire.

Fear not what others think.
Drive hard, drive fast!
Keep your eyes on the horizon.

Stay young inside.
Don't let Troubles age you before time is tasked with doing so.

Let enemies walk away.
Ignore fear.

listen to your mother and father.
They should know more about fear and should be able to teach us
how to move passed it before we grow to old
and scared in our youth.

We are young.

Troubles will always be...

It's up to us to kill them while we're still strong enough to do so.
If we allow Troubles to get us down now, than we'll never get up again.
The time to fight is now.
The time to hold tight is now.

Chase the dreams and remember your shadows.
Keep watch over your heart.

Let Go before the Universe Puts you Down.

It's time to let go or drown in tears, blood and fighting.
Something inside is conflicting with the external.
Nothing is adding up, everything is off.
I'm on tilt.

The universe is trying to tell me something.
My friends have seen it.
They all agree, something isn't right.
I've tried, fought, given, lived and died to much for things to be the way they are now.
I'm not in-line with the events of my life.
Tomorrow has no plan for me.
I have breached too far beyond my original goals.
Today is fighting me with everything.

I see the signs now.
This city isn't good for me.
Money is an issue.
The law is an issue.
Love has been pushed aside.
But still I try to push forward.

I can see now that I've been pushing forward in the wrong direction.

I'm off course. So off course that it took me this long to realize that my compass is broke.
If things were in order I wouldn't be in this life.
I wouldn't be.....
here
I'd be happier.
I'd be somewhere that I still felt whole.

I've lost myself.
Not to drugs.
Not to drink.
Not to addictions.
I've lost myself in life.
I need to take control again.
Time is too short to let this fly on auto pilot anymore.

I'm writing out my dreams.
My goals.
My childhood fantasies.
It's time to realign myself with the cosmos.

I'm letting go.
Turning around.
Going back to the starting position.
But not going home.

There's no longer a need to hang on to this.
Everything is against me.
If I go any further down this path I will surely be dropped off a cliff and left to fall forever more.

WC Chambers

pretty in pink

My string of pink pearls snaps in half.
I watch the pink pearls fall to the floor
like bubbles bursting when they drift down to pavement.
The pearl beads fly everywhere
as the frayed thread holding them together breaks.
The pink silk bow on my t-shirt unties, exposes a red patchy scar
wrapped up like a Christmas present.
People have told me I look like Molly Ringwald in "Pretty in Pink."
But I'm not going to prom.
I'm at the Race for the Cure,
walking a mile in pink canvas tennis shoes bedazzled with
rhinestones,
spray painted the color of cotton candy.
Eating cotton candy is fun
but marching in this clown parade feels more like an obligation,
a debt I owe to the universe to be a fundraiser
just because I lost a breast,
just because I lost a pound of pink flesh,
just because I gritted my teeth
through six months of chemotherapy six weeks of radiation 12
months of Herceptin and five hours of mastectomy.
I feel like I've got something to prove,
that I can still walk, that I can still move,
so I'm marching in this one mile "fun" walk
with the other pink soldiers in a circle around Linn Park,
stepping into muddy puddles,
splattering my cotton candy shoes,
and clouding my rhinestones with murky clay
before I pose by the pink fountain for a picture,
proud of my pink lip gloss that glitters,
pink eye shadow that sparkles,
and pink headband to match my pink "survivor" t-shirt.

As I pose for this picture after the pink clown parade,
the stereo speakers blast "I hope you dance"
from the ceremonies stage.
And I happen to shoot a glance to where my mother sits.
She's crying
'cause she never wanted a daughter of hers to go through this.
And frankly, I wish I hadn't marched in this survivors' parade,
patting myself on the back for surviving something that chose me,
giving myself a trophy just for getting out of bed
and breathing.
I survived breast cancer. So?
Hell no! I wanna win a hundred bucks at a poetry slam,
I wanna win first place in a battle I picked
And I wanna come to that battle all dressed in black.
Give me a pair of scissors
so I can cut this pink ribbon
binding my flesh and hurting my back.
Give me a felt tip marker
so I can paint my tennis shoes black.
I wanna untie this pink ribbon presenting me as a pretty package,
I wanna pull this thread dangling from the edge
of my pink "survivor" t-shirt.
I want these t-shirt threads to unravel, fall apart
so you can see this patchy red scar
slithering across my chest like a snake.
I want you to see this clay vessel the potter plays with on his pottery wheel.
This battle has broken me, scarred and deformed me.
A pound of pink flesh has been extracted from me
just so I can get out of bed
and breathe.
But this wrestling match has not transformed me.
I am not Jacob who wrestled with God and walked away blessed.
I walked away from this battle looking like Shrek
with green, ogre-like toenails fungal from chemo
covered in cotton candy shoes

Photo by Rosie Lindsey

bedazzled with rhinestones
to match my pink lip gloss that glitters.
All that glitters isn't gold or silver.
I transform myself into what society wants to see—
a breast cancer survivor all pretty in pink
but this pink ribbon
disguises a monster standing before me in the mirror
and this prosthesis-stuffed bra
stops the snake on my chest from being able to slither.

Lori Lasseter Hamilton

#trauma

There are times we are victims to the worst humanity has to offer, and there is no rhyme or reason behind it. While it may take years to get over the pain, and while we will never again be the same, the fact that we are still here and brave enough to tell our story is a testament to our strength, and survival skills.

Cry

What does it say about this world of ours
that the first reaction of any human born into it
is to CRY.
We take our first breaths, all of us, and if we are healthy,
we shriek into this new world,
bloodcurdling and reassuring just the same
because this is the human thing.
No other creature on this planet does it.
The new mother anxiously awaits that wailing
tell-tale sign that her little one
has firmly set foot this side of the cosmic curtain—
"Listen to him scream!" she says, "He's a strong one!"
Flash forward five years to the playground
where the bullies' taunts tear the tears from his eyes.
Now Mama says, "Big boys don't cry."
Don't cry.
Don't cry?
Don't follow this instinct that comes as naturally as breathing?
Why not cry?
Why not celebrate tears of all flavors?
Sadness, fear, joy, love—
any emotion that overflows.
So, go ahead, baby,
cry.
Cry for all the hearts out there,
beating, bleeding, broken, uninhibited and on the sleeve,
restless, lonely, artificial... diseased.
Cry.
But don't cry alone.
Gather together in pairs, groups, crowds.
Fill the open spaces, grasp each other like family,
gaze into the eyes of a stranger.

Opposite: "Skin Deep" by TM Rhyno

Know eachother to be kinfolk conjoined at the soul.
Let all your shoulders be wet and weighted down
with the tears of your brothers and sisters.
Go ahead, join them and
cry—
for injustice, nevermind the latitude or longitude,
the language, color of skin
or local nickname for God.
In all dialects, a wail of pain is still the same
and the whimpers of the oppressed are unmistakable.
Translate these sounds and cry,
bittersweet tears for the strong,
because tonight she decided to leave him.
He will never touch her again.
Cry out in anger, but don't forget to also
cry for joy
because someone, somewhere
just felt the first kick and is choosing a name
that will outlive her.
She will bear down & give birth to the future with a cry.
One day "daddy's little girl"
will run away beneath a shower of rice,
tears falling on asphalt like spring rain
behind those rattling cans.
Cry—
for other futures that never quite unfurl.
Mothers that rock slowly in silent rooms,
air unbroken by any cries
other than their own,
as they hold good little babies
who will never wake them at 3am
and will never,ever cry.
The world is mostly ocean,
salty just like tears and
whatever we are on the outside—

we all cry.
Cry for her.
Cry for him.
Cry me a river and lets all swim.
Don't hide your face
when you bless your cheeks with
those drops of grace.
No matter what you've been told—
there is no shame in crying.

D. Victory

forgiveness

I've been trying to diet into
a ten year forgiveness high school reunion suit
chest out
gut in
back straight
the past will not give room for breath

the past
classified compartmentalized conversations
consolation lock with consoling key

ssshhhhhhh
a lovers finger
pressed against a whisper

the past unpacks itself
in the damnedest of places
in a daughters hand searching for security

the past carries itself
opens up
in a coworkers cup of coffee

here's a six year old black boy in a body bag
his cousins put him there
stuffed a cock in his mouth
when his innocence tried to breathe

a twelve year old black boy in a body bag
wished himself to sleep after realizing
hunger and abandonment
were not imaginary friends

but closer than play cousins
not caring if mommy caught them kissing

A nineteen year old black boy in a body bag
We actually ran a special that day
Three triggers
A half a dozen fatherless teenagers
Confusing manhood with being real niggers

the past won't ask for forgiveness
there's power in the grip
holding on to hatred
giving power to the hatred
allowing a tighter grip
on everything that happen in the past
that we blame ourselves for
when the actions of others
made us feel powerless

The fatal flaw of feeling like damaged goods
It's not that the past will kill you
But carrying all that baggage
Will not allow you to live

They say when water falls from the sky
While parted clouds allows the sun to shine
The devil is crying

We are here to live
To turn demons into summer rain
And dance with them in the sunshine

I mean really live
life can monkey tribe hurricane
crap from all directions

It's the one smiling
In the eye of a dime a dozen shit storm
Whose worth knowing

I got a friend
Who whenever the world seems
All hellfire and brimstone
Fingers a heart shaped halo
Reminding herself
That in our darkest hours
We are all angels needing love

Love more times than not
Comes in forgiveness dresses, and
reconciliation suits
Sized too small to fit our true selves
with our past

Our flesh is not a body bag
Meant to carry the dead weight of yesterday
Our skin is forgiveness
Proof that we are still here

The past is not sustenance
Strengthening our bones
Its rigor mortis
moving from the big toe
to the myocardium
consuming every bit of life
we hide in bodies

let go of the grip on the baggage
let yourself feel the forgiveness
of your skin holding you tight

the 19 year old black boy
realizes it's not his fault
some men aren't man enough
to be daddy
so he has to be the father he wants for his children
to himself

starting with resurrecting the six year old black boy
forgiving himself for being sexually powerless
the twelve year old
forgiving himself
for not having control over external existing circumstances

there is no room for the past in our skins
forgiveness is nightmare bullet proof
only leaving space for the lovers
we need to be
to ourselves

Christopher Johnson

Move Slow

In the places
I have lived
lives, nine
times ninety,
the places and
the lives
numbers that
shame felines,
(The things
that I have done.
the same feelings,
shame.)
in these places
things move
slow.
Slow as steam
from a gut-pile
left hunter fresh
on November
mornings
in Arkansas woods.
Slow as crows
feast, for thanksgiving
until no evidence
remains.
At nineteen,
up North with
an uncle,
days spent
breaking back
and mopping
hot tar

I learned this
most valuable
lesson of all
in a bar called
Lost Acres
outside of Chicago,
on the Joliett side.
I met a guy
named Lucky
he had white hair,
a quick grin
and a small fleet
of trucks.
He rode a
Knucklehead Harley,
was clever,
and smooth with
ladies. He was
everything
I had always
pretended to be.
Lucky moved slow.
He took me
to Kings Shoeshines,
hooked me up
with dark ladies
whose tits
had cost more
than my car,
he drove me to
Cicero and showed
me where
to cop dope.
The first bag
on him.

The lesson
didn't stick though
until he asked
a pistol favor,
my debt weighing
heavy in hand.
In moments
like these
things move slow,
because you
don't just ask
a guy
to kill someone
all at once.

Justin Booth

Communion

*If the wine change into vinegar and the host crumble into corruption
after they have been consecrated, is Jesus Christ still present under
their species as God and as man?*
-James Joyce

drip
       drop into holy water
  blood bath, drool spills
from words tucked under tongue
take the cup, drink the wine, turn the dime
     from donation basket panhandlers
     "thank you for your contribution
     to our parish"
     my child, my lamb
     so quiet, so tame
censored by wine
spirit and mind
lie down
for the father
        open your mouth
        for daddy
          that's it
          wider
            good boy–
now kneel and close
your eyes my child
submit
senses
     now eat my flesh
     my palimpsest
       break my skin
       with your teeth

let me put it
in your mouth
      tuck your words
      under your tongue
            repent your thoughts
            open your heart

      come back
            black eyes

you are forgiven   welcome
back
you are reborn
my child

Evan Bryant Patton

Precipitation

I've seen the rains of changes
come crashing down in torrential waves

But it had been awhile for me

it had been awhile
since I've felt the rains of change
wash down these cheeks
it had to have been a few decades or more
not since I was no more then four.

I thought I grew immune to the tears,
(big boys don't cry, big boys don't cry)
I couldn't imagine I'd ever hear
the tune of this grown up man
crying
mourning
& breaking down

But one day, one day the clouds in me
threatened to finally break free
As the blowing winds stroked my parched cheeks,
and the skies began to crumble
the lightning ripping thru to those
broken dreams,
stolen things,
used to be's,
woe's are me's

and once the rains came they didn't stop
they started with a drip and a drop

drip drop
drip drop drip drop

And I cried for all the things I failed to shed tears for—drip
I cried 34 years worth—drop
I cried all those held back tears—drip
I cried for childhood fears—drop
I cried for the the ones that used to care—drip
I cried for the long lost years—drop
I cried for world despairs—drip
I cried for the dearly departed—drop
I cried for the gone good-hearted—drip
I cried for the disappearing dreams—drop
I cried just for me—drip

I cried just for me—drop

And I cried

I cried for all I was

drip drop

And I cried

I cried for all I am

drip drop

And I cried

I cried for all I will be

drip drop

And I cried

drip drop drip drop drip drop drip drop drip drop
drip drop drip drop drip drop drip drop

til finally the rain ripped a hole in my sky
and all I could do to stay sane
was keep on crying
and oh how I tried
to stop the storm
but it kept on coming for more
and I kept on crying

drip drop

the tears rolled down my cheeks
in streams, in rivers, in crashing waves
pounding on my shores

drip drop

and my once parched cheeks
welcomed these rains of change
and as each one fell it relieved the pain
that I kept so deep inside me
until finally

I let go
I released my hold
I opened my soul
to the raining skies inside

drip drop

I let go
I allowed the clouds to open up
I welcomed the storm
I let the rain drops flow

and fall from my eyes
and my once dried up, thirsty baby blues
took on a different hue
as they swam in these streams
from these rains
washing down my cheeks

drip drop

each one falling from me—drip
calling to me—drop
reminding me—drip
that this storm is—drop
healing me—drip
releasing me—drop
cleansing me—drip
opening me—drop
baptizing me—drip
freeing me—drop

and the drips and the drops
of this internal storm
began to stop

drip

and the sky opened

drop

and the sun shined down
upon me

once again

Johnny Olson

A Perfect Storm

Storm clouds gathered around me
From before my birth,
One night stand, unexpected pregnancy,
Mom's college career ended suddenly,
Forecast called for heavy rains,
Tough choices to be made.
Pressured to hide away—secret adoption—
Marrying a stranger
Her only other option;
She did it for me.
But lightning does strike
The same place twice,
A father and an uncle
Each bringing power outages
Into my life
With their electrical discharge,
But I reply!
No longer voiceless,
I thunder,
And with the strength of the wind
Behind my words,
I will be heard.
Scattered squalls chatter
About "inappropriate subject matter,"
But what is inappropriate here
Is to survive these hurricanes
That swallow little girls whole
And shipwreck their souls
Only to be told
Just to "keep it on the down low."

But I,
I am a perfect storm now,
And this tsunami in my eyes
Will rise
To overflow and sweep away
The walls of shame and silence.

Jerri Hardesty

Open Letter:
I Will Rename Us

No One Understands not even me
When the media
Blared your crime and my punishment
I dropped the stone they placed in my hand
became your announcing ghost

What did we do for the duppy
To come in our door
Jiggling coins in a pouch
A glass of rum in her hand
The wind shivering
In a crème brulee sky

It's a sickness, just when I'm cured, the cancer spreads
Hydra without Iphicles to slay it
A vicious cycle pain on pain
celery colored bruise on an arm
persimmon mark on a cheek
blue sage shadow on a thigh

Left on many occasions, just to return
They say why do you stay
My heart the latchkey
That allowed strangers in my house
leaving debris and excuses
Tisiphone, my avenger
Was not accepting calls that day

Black Pearl, I rename you

woman whose voice sounds like a tear
your dark skin cast before so many
comfort men and woman
carrying centuries on our backs
Sirocco I rename us

Gayle Bell

Ape Bite

It is not major. I was bit by
an ape once. A tiny ape,
malaysian.

Wasn't messing with it,
was drinking cola, ape
bit through my fingertips
on my right hand.

I screamed;
bites are deadly,
if it had disease, if I get disease,
if I spread the disease
and cause pandemic?

The police said it was
common
said they did not
euthanize apes

On both counts, I hope they
were not telling the truth.

Grant Leuning

No.

Monsters coveting space
under my bed
resting upon my nightmare stained pillow
every ounce of forced flesh
scars already so deep
buried underneath my true beauty
large palm to forehead
lowering sacrament to places demons refuse
to linger
submissive
learned screaming does nothing
only causes more silence
anger suppresses itself
waving around white flags
hands are inscribed with darkness
it sleeps
lives in a barrel of broken sighs
tears slip
frightened,
my hands have spent hours trembling
knowing I will share my bed with no man
who will ever understand
or accept

Sometimes I come unfolded.

He asks/He thinks

How many times did they hurt you?
Why did you let them?
How many mouths trespassed on your skin?
Why didn't you say no?

How many hands tried to break you?
Why didn't you fight back harder?

How many cocks ripped into your body?
Why didn't you scream?
How many teeth marks did they leave?
Why didn't you bite back?
Did any draw blood?
Why didn't you set their houses on fire?

I reply
I did not ask for any of this.
I said NO.
I tried to fight.
I kicked.

I choked on my own tears,
and voice.
I bit until my gums bled.
I can still feel the salt on my tongue.

I didn't have any matches.

Jennifer E. Hudgens

This Poem

I don't know if I can write this poem.
It's the one about my father:
About his warm eyes of ocean blue
Spilling kindness,
Always generous,
Broad sense of humor with belly laughs,
His skill with a guitar,
California Dreaming in the early morning hour—
The way he liked to have sex with his daughter.

I don't know if I should write this poem.
The accusation kept silent for so long,
The past is the past
And so far gone,
But I was Daddy's dirty little secret,
And that label lives on.

I don't know if I could write this poem.
Because words could never in justice describe
The pain in a little girl's eyes,
Not just mine,
But millions of girls throughout time,
Daddy's little girls,
Betrayed and defiled,
Left to wrestle those demons inside
For the rest of their lives.

I don't know if I would write this poem.
'Cause, see, I've always focused my poetry
On the positive side,
On the power and peace found inside,
And pushed the pain aside,

But now I've opened my eyes,
And I've seen those girls, like me,
With a schism in their lives.
I have met them:
On the streets,
In the schools,
At the poetry slams.

I don't know if I will write this poem.
But now, I know I want to!
I want to enfold those sister girls
Into strong arms
And together cry because they say,
"Daddies are the only men little girls can trust,"
But not for us,
Our love twisted into perverted knots.
And the catch-22 here
Is that I still don't forgive myself,
And yet I see in those other's eyes
Reflected guilt,
Soul's windows clouded shut,
And I want to cry out
That theirs is not the shame
That theirs is not the blame,
But belongs to the one who gave them a name.
And that man is the blueprint
By which we judge all other men we meet,
Leaving us handicapped,
Unable to find what they need.
And it's not just Fathers.
It's uncles, and cousins, and brothers,
Even Mothers:
Those who should protect,
Forsake.

I don't know if I can write this poem.
But I know I cannot forget
Those silent nights,
Those nightmare frights,
Of little girls tonight.
And I know this is short on metaphor,
And I know I don't have that hip-hop score,
But forget all that,
Because this is something more,
And I've never ranted or raved or sworn
In my poetry before,
But these girls I speak of,
They're all around you, even now.
And we know who we are,
We bear the internal scar,
The one that's so hard to heal
Because it was with us from the start,
And it is for them
That I know I must write this poem.

Jerri Hardesty

Jock Dates Drummer.

She showed you that you are made
of bones and empty spaces, like any
instrument, like any slender girl. She played you—
kept beat on your hollow stomach with her palm,
rapped crude rhythm in knuckles on your sternum.

The sixteenth time someone said,
Are you fucking that drummer girl?
you were not surprised.

You never changed in the track locker room. Alone
in the bathroom stall, no one could shy away from your
gaze,
ask you about the bruises that bloomed
like eighth notes along your ribs.
In practice, pain is irrelevant.
You were never safer
than in uniform, indistinguishable
from other girls at a distance.

Someone should have told you
what it means to carry
your bones, the worst of you
so near the surface; someone should have
told you to keep your fists up.

Logen Cure

Suicide Aftermath

Why couldn't I read her despair
like I read my books?

I saw the dark shadows
creeping up between the lines
but felt helpless
to change the storyline.

The plot was an old one—
a bitter childhood,
mental illness
and the wish to be something
she never could achieve.

I could see the climax coming
as the characters
slowly drifted apart.
But how was I to know
that the end would come early
and by her own hand?

This drama, has officially
become a tragedy
and the narrator
is now the villain.

Maranda Russell

Today

Today
I impersonated a magnificent poet
and this! This is my tribute to him.
Today
I reached into the back of my brain
under cobwebs and dust
and found boxes of storage,
but I decided to leave them there for now.
Today
I learned new words like
sedulous, divestiture, and indelibility
so that I can take a test
that puts a number
on my ability to analytically regurgitate
ponderous vocabulary.
Today
I lived in a homeless shelter
with desperate men and women
who have simply been unlucky
or imprudent
and I knew that I belonged there.
Today
was greatest day of my life
but I missed it
because I was looking elsewhere.
Today
I drank half a bottle of cheap whiskey
then took a handful of pills
while he watched me
and then I realized I didn't want to die
I just wanted to know if he cared,
and I had my answer.

Today
a voice asked me, "What is your name?"
and I shushed the voice
because I didn't know what to say.
Today
I got new glasses
and the world is less fuzzy than before.
Today
I drew a picture of an empty hallway
lit with fluorescent bulbs
and open windows
and it was a good drawing.
Today
a hand tightly grasped my throat
and I was commanded to take off my clothes
or else I would die
and I believed him and followed his orders
because my life is more valuable
than my dignity.
Today
those who swear to serve and protect
chose not to believe me
because I don't bruise easily.
Today
I was held securely by a beautiful man
but time is short and space is far
and I may never be held so safely again.
Today
I comprehended the difference
between having sex
and making love.
Today
my entire body felt like pins and needles
and there wasn't a damn thing
I could do about it.

Today
I wanted to see the apartment
where my husband and I first lived
but instead I found a parking lot
and I was glad that it had been torn down
just like our marriage.
Today
I miss my best friend,
every single best friend I've ever had
who has come and gone for whatever reason
and I wished I could undo things done
unlisten to things heard
and unspeak things said
just to have them back.
Today
I want to tell my daughter
that I love her
and that she is not like me.
Today
I am no longer suicidal
but I kill myself a little each day.
Today
was the day of my birth
and I immediately started wasting time
wishing for impossible things
and trusting too much.
Today
some things don't change.

Lilly Penhall

take your seat please/ playground marbles

Paul?

Yes Mrs Heinz.

You were late today.

Yes Mrs Heinz.

We've discussed this before so I'd like you to stay in at recess and write the class a poem

But..

then tomorrow you can read it to us.

But..

That'll be all for now. Take your seat please.

Yes Mrs Heinz.

Playground Marbles

I have the most.
And I am the best. And I am brave.

I am the best marble player in school.

I keep my playground marbles

in a drawstring pouch.
The pouch looks like bit-o-honey
or captain crunch
or the color of the sun
sitting in a wheatfield.

During recess we all run out to play.

The playground is asphalt.

Where the asphalt ends
and before the grass begins
there is good even dirt.
This is where we dig.
And we dig to catch the marbles.
And we dig to see who's best.

The hole we dig is the size of a tuna can.

The Earth is soft and brown like my Mother's hair.

In my pouch I have purees and steelies
and cats-eyes and swirlies.
I have rubies and greenies and blues.
I have the most. And I am the best. And I am brave.

On my stomach and in the dirt my fingers are perfect.

And they know who invented marbles.
And they know the answer to the capital of Vermont.
And they know long division.
And they know the right thing to say when Dad asks
why you havent finished raking all the leaves yet
(middle finger extended).

Then one day that little weasel
Andy Eyerise stole my marble pouch.

I ran to Mrs Heinz
but all she said was
"take your seat please."

Now all my marbles are gone
and I have to go home and explain to my Dad
that all the marbles he bought me are gone.

And I am not brave anymore.

School day done
head hung low
homeward I trudged.

Kicking rocks and praying my father would be out

I found him sitting
at the kitchen table
eating creamed hamburger on toast
he called shit-on-a-shingle.

Hoping to pass unnoticed
I also prayed for invisibility.

And he stopped eating his favorite meal.
And he looked up.
And he looked me in the eye.

And God can see where you are weak.

And my Father asked "where are all your marbles?"
And I told him.

And he said "rest your hand on the table palm up."

And he
walked out of
the kitchen and
down the basement steps.

Moments later he returned
holding his hands behind his back
and said "pick one."

I wished for steelies or rubies.

In a way
both hands held
something steel and something red.

And I picked
his left-hand
because he was a lefty.

And the glint of metal
reminded me of the special
fillet knives he kept in the basement.

And I've always thought
my thin white scar
looked like a crooked little smile.

You asked me for a poem.
And all I brought you was a handful of pain.

Two for flinching.

Paul Koniecki

One-Night Fosters

Everything in the Riverside chapter is the dingy white
of eggshells two half flights up in an off-base military flat,
Roni and me lying in bed in the streetlight pall, scanning
faraway stations on rocket ship shaped radios

tryin' to drown out Daddy's worthless and send you backs
and Momma's muffled don't want tos, our curtains waving
in change on summer California breeze, breaking our happy
all the way hell as I give up and fight for sleep.

Over my head, I hear music in the air...

That chorus I'd just memorized plays in louder than out-
of-range station static; and I see folding chairs on a concrete drive,
a little blond woman with puffy hair pacing 'tween rows
of folding chairs, leather book swinging, trying to sing

Jesus into slap-happy Air Force kids who'd come to her
driveway vacation Bible school every day for two weeks.
She served pretzels, cookies, chocolate milk and
something to do at least an hour a day in old hot Boringland.

Didn't hear music but took her word for it,
cut my story book cutouts, glued baby Moses
to his basket, floated him downriver, into
those famous rushes and some handmaiden's waiting hands

the way we find ourselves shuttled off the next day into
strange beds for the night while Dad goes off, unexplained,
Momma in tow. No goodbyes, no explanations, just PJs
and a dark room, music playing from beyond the door.

Over my head, I hear music in the air...

Think I'm dreaming, really, when the door swings wide,
back-lit shadow walking toward me with a stagger, says,
Here. Take this. Something smooth, warm, mostly round,
a soft ridge wrapping round it, and a soft dip at the center.

You want to see your daddy again, put this in your mouth,
me at eight years old, oblivious to anything that means,
I touch it again and think I've no idea where here is and
heck if I'm gonna stay someplace with little hard beds,

mean ol' kids who whine about giving up their room and
surely will get us back for that when no one's looking.
Do it, comes that voice, or you'll never see your momma
or your daddy again, as my eyes adjust slowly to the light.

This is not pretzels, cookies or chocolate anything, but
I sure as heck ain't staying' in this strange dark place.
So I lean in, and Roni's voice is not Roni from 'cross the room,
says, No! Don't do it, Rosie, as the door opens again

and some woman's pulling Dark And Scary struggling
from the room, leaving me confused. There's hell to pay
from the sound of things out in the hallway, that woman
slapping Dark And Scary 'round with newspaper or a paddle

and Roni out of bed peeking out at them before she shuts the door.
If he does that again you bite him. She crawls back into bed.
We listen as the slapping stops and Dark And Scary's voice
moves off into the distance, back to bein' Daddy's Air Force friend.

Over my head, I hear music in the air.
There must be a God somewhere.

Rose M. Smith

Desecrated

A knocking at my door.
Twelve thirty 'ish on a Friday night.
Canceled plans...
Sleeping.
Groggily get up,
Stumble to the door,
Look out the peephole.
A friend,
Standing with a 6 pack of beer
In his hands.
Told him;
"Ray's not here."
Reply:
"That's cool."
Sure, why not?
many night's spent
drinking cold ones,
Swimming in the pool,
soaking in the hot tub.
Good memories.
Why not make more?

Everything good.
Until after the first beer,
When he began to push himself
On me.
Grabbing my breasts and
Trying to unbutton my pants.
Forcing me down onto the couch.
Leaning on me with all his weight
as he tore the clothes from my body.

I kept telling him, "No, I don't want to do this!!! Please stop!"
I tried fighting him, but he was too big...
 too strong.
He grabbed a handful of hair,
Pulled my head back
And told me if I
"didn't give him what he wanted,"
He "might kill me!"
I thought:
"what the hell, a little bit of puss?
Better than dying, right?"
It wasn't like I hadn't had sex before.
I had no idea he would take...
so much more...

He held me down as he forced himself into me.
The violation...
The tears...
The pain...
Encompassed my soul.
Threatened to overwhelm my very being.
I shut my eyes;
Prayed he would hurry,
Finish,
So he could leave me...
Alive.

After about 10 minutes of pounding,
Grunting, and thrusting, he finally finished,
Got off of me...
I lie there with my eyes closed
Until I heard the slamming of the door.
Quickly jumping up,
 locking the door
behind him.

Collapsing in a heap to the floor...
Sobbing uncontrollably...
slowly crawling to the shower,
Where I stood,
Blood running down my legs,
Purplish-blue bruises on my breasts,
fingerprint bruises on my thighs, my arms, my breasts, my throat.
A red mark across my cheek where he had struck me...
Compulsively trying to erase any evidence
Of him
On, and within, my body.
The feeling of being
Oh so dirty...filthy
Of never ever being clean again.
The soul tarnished, impure.
I could not tell
Where my tears ended
And the water droplets began.

(post script?)
For six years,
I never told a soul...
No-one.
Vowed to forget it myself
As if it never happened.

6 years later, a next door neighbor confided
She had been raped
Beaten severely
And left for dead on the
Side of a road.
Haunted memories
Flooded my consciousness.
How did I know her feelings?

That night slowly came back...
Pain enveloping my soul
once again.
Consciously dealing with it
Allowed me to heal
And in the process,
Allowed her to heal.

Terri Black

Monster

In six days God created the heavens and the earth.
He rested on the Sabbath day.
God blessed the Sabbath day.
God's first day off.
This must have been when monsters were created.

I think I was about 10 years old.
I'd go in Daddy's room, open the bottom drawer,
Set his folded work pants aside and I found the prize...
Those little books.
No pictures, so an active imagination necessary.
Yeah, this freak that stands before you was being formed.
But this literary porn confused me because
When it spoke of couples making love,
He would kiss her lips and the nape of her neck and I'd ask myself:
"How can he kiss her while having sex?"
I couldn't picture this in my mind because, remember, you
Taught me sex was just one person doing it to another from behind.

I looked at sex then almost as I do now.
It was special.
With someone you loved and trusted.
It was always finished in the bed and started out in the bathtub.
Now I call it making love,
But when I was 8, I called it being raped by you,
My favorite male cousin.

God's second day off.

The Sabbath... never felt so unholy.

Disregarding my skinny, little body didn't belong to you,

You went in and out as you pleased.
I guess with no hymen to speak of,
You chose to tear my self esteem up.
Got to the point that I hated to see you coming so much so
That I actually liked to feel you come inside me
Because that meant it was over.
How many more unholy Sabbaths would you force me to endure?
Obviously the monsters I thought were in my closet
Were the least of my worries because you... never came out of yours.
And the scary part is you didn't have an affinity for men...
Just this little kid.

Oh yeah, you liked baths,
Which must be why you made me take them two,
Sometimes three times a day.
Did you know that I only take showers now?
Because a bath is only asking for another bad Sabbath.
Sometimes I wanna ask you who in heaven was on the take
For you to know ALL of my guardian angel's coffee breaks.
Because while God was taking a nap, or fishing,
Or whatever it is God does when He has the day off,
You were force feeding me the word 'faggot'
With stabbing thrusts down my throat,
Making me think I was the one who wanted it
When I didn't know that I did nothing wrong and it wasn't my fault.
And how could questions about my sexuality NOT cross my mind
When it took porn to teach me that there was more to sex
Than forced blowjobs and doggy-style?
And I'm not bashing gays, cousin, because you were NOT a homosexual.

You were a freakin' devil.

A demon that possessed and raped me repeatedly
During the many unholy Sabbaths you made come two,
Sometimes three times a week.

And I'm not a man.
Just a 34 year old boy who still avoids you
At family gatherings and reunions and
Out of sheer fear, still locks the door when I go to the bathroom
And almost had a panic attack that one time someone broke the lock
So you tell me…
…why'd God have to take so many days off?

In Exodus 20:8, God said to remember the Sabbath because He called it blessed.
But you've shown me monsters don't have to remember,
So you tell me…
How can I forget?

Tavis P. Brunson

Opposite: Painting by A Nero

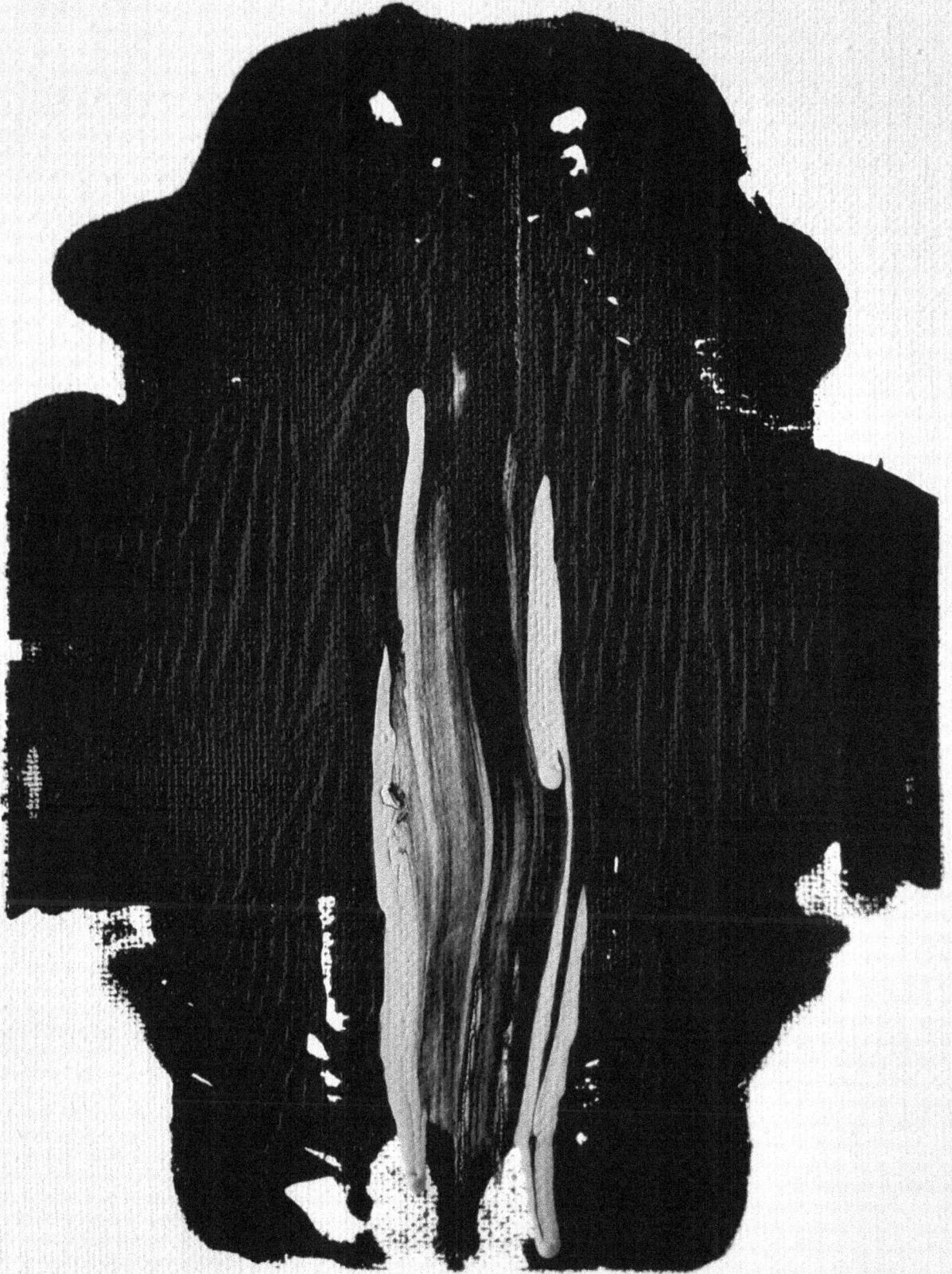

#demons

There is a battle raging inside each and every one of us,
as we struggle to overcome whatever demons may beset
us. But no matter what type of demon we are tormented
by, if we can find a way to cope with, or beat our demons,
we prove that even if we don't always win, that we are
determined enough to survive to fight the good fight.

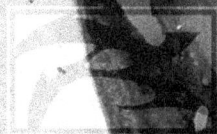

Sometimes a bullet looks pretty good

There is a raging battle with
Dark emotional demons
Sometimes it cant be helped
Creature of logic
Fumbling over the reasoning
The poet doesn't ask to feel deeper
Love harder, or see clearer
The poet doesn't ask to fight injustice
He is compelled to do these things
Obsess over sentences, life, and love.
Sometimes the poet doesn't even choose to be a poet
Usually it just comes more natural than blinking
Second nature just like a heartbeat or sunrise
There are periods of frantic creativity
The words come faster than the fingers can move
There are manic days of creative dryness
He doubts if he's even a poet, although he knows he was meant to be.
Sometimes poetry is the only thing that keeps him alive
Sometimes a bullet looks pretty good in the face of
Failure. Poets sing, dance, write, paint, drive, fight, fuck
Drink, and drug. And that is the short list.
We are beaten humanity's voice
When no one will speak against the tyranny
Of society. When no one will rage and fight
Or hold and love.
When you are down to your last beer
and there's no where to sleep,
a poet will welcome you home.

Desmene Statum

Gainful Employment

I used to think I'd find
Work that paid me to
Drink and take drugs
The CIA, or maybe DEA.
Some team of ultra-cool agents
And their square jawed
Buzz cit boss would say
"Well boys, we don't know what this does,
But the Kids are crazy for it
Go get the Geek."
And there I'd be
Pulled from some weird
Infinitely large sci-fi library
With books by PKD
He would have written
If he hadn't died prematurely
And other such wonders
Like video games
On holographic light displays
They'd bring me Mushrooms in baskets
Stimulants and acid
Bags of weed with no last hit
They'd bring me knock-off prescriptions
Clean needles and pipes
All the keys to endless nights
Bootleg whiskey and vodka
All the glory, none of the fall
Those nice cops
Would offer the season's best
Chemical crop
They'd hug on me and love on me
Never a risk of being shot

My god wouldn't it just be awesome
Didn't get recruited though
Too bad, coulda given
A really big show
A really big show
Instead, serial soul killing jobs
I was a surly waiter
A poor line-cook
Packed boxes in warehouses
Even drove forklifts
Till I damaged so much shit
That my bosses got pissed
And moved me back to boxes
Before firing me a week later
Or maybe I quit, like I always did
Then there was the year I spent
In kevlar chaps, chainsaw in hand
Cutting thick brush back
From the miles of Alabama power-lines
In the cold and the rain
In the heat and the sweat
I'll never forget
Tripping down that hill
Revved blade held tight,
Didn't let go, don't know why
Chain grinding my thigh
The night before I'd gotten high
Crack off a beer-can pipe
Had no sleep, should have died
That trick was neat
'Cause kevlar chaps
Don't cover arms or eyes
Throats, fingers, nor feet
Stopped the tumble at the base
Kevlar fibers flying up into

My miraculously intact face
You'd think a boy could learn
But it wasn't 10 days astern
When I stopped my own heart
With an IV shot o' cocaine
8, 12, 16, 20
Beats or more
The stillness of my pump
Was the coldness of the void
My blood had stopped moving
But the most beautiful train
Was rushing through my brain
Rocketing through my head
Ba-dump, ba, ba-dump. ba
My heart starts to beat
Once again, not dead
Wish I coulda said
I changed right then
But it took another month
Of degradation and pain
Till I called Mom in Kentucky
And begged for help
Thus began the long climb
Up all those hills
I'd always fallen down
Many pratfalls and slips
Between then and now
To stand here
On this solid ground
To become a man
With a job that rewards
A sweet, smart, beautiful wife
In short, a man with a life
Worth living
Don't do much now

That needs forgiving
So give me the mike
If you like
What I speak now
Though tried and true
Is both eternal and brand new

Brad Wood

Five Years.

I'm living my life in a cycle of self-hatred
Where did this begin and where does it end?
Controlled by my desires, I have to seek a measure of change
Five years ago when we first met, it was simple.
Now I hardly know myself

You promised excitement and you delivered. Boy, did you ever
But everything changes with time and so have I
My life was an open book and there were no secrets.
Anyone could see
Now I'm wondering if I'll ever break these chains

I never fell for your friends,
those you run with so shamelessly
You were available. Easy. Cheap. Harmless. Harmless?
So I ran with your crowd and along for the ride of my life
I was captivated
For three years I ignored the signs now I don't think I'll overcome

Every afternoon I wake to the same argument with myself
I will not see you today. My feet will not grace your step.
Then once in your living room, drinking tea and reminiscing, I am ashamed.
They talk of my potential but now I know I'll forever disappoint.

I almost found a reason to break it off, another love. An honorable endeavor.
Yet returning to your arms, I am your slave
I've kept you a secret (you still are to most) and carried on
For months I've lied to myself and now I need you to be what you were

Be what you were or get out of my life!
Is there a solution or will I die in your bed?
I'm turning the page to an unwritten chapter and what will they write of this day?
"Five years was a long time but he finally got away"

Eric Blackerby

Untitled

I.

She's a pure personality
with no chemical additives
I envy this
as I envy the seed
that lands in fertile soil
it is the will of the wind
and you cannot bribe the breeze
my only option
was to take root in loose gravel
and push my way through rocks
to have a shot at the sun
she was born in a garden
well-kept and weeded daily
allowed to grow unencumbered
and fully ripen
under the protection of scarecrows
and green thumbs
again
I envy this
but am learning to respect the seedling
that battled boulders and droughts
battled the rocky burial
of her beginning
and still touched the same sovereign sky
to smile back at the sun

II.

You must think I'm a goldfish
with a memory that resets
like a sunrise
every day is a clean slate
for you to scuff up
and scribble your anger on
you've stopped asking for
forgiveness
or committing your lips
to an apology
you've spun unconditional love
into uneasy obligation
and I hate expectations

III.

When I needed traction the most
you gave me sleet
and covered your eyes
as I spun out of control

IV.

I was barely grown
when I consumed my first
unnecessary pill
popping a prison term
by mistake
I served a full dime
before I saw the sun again

V.

Does it get any better than this
a slick grey morning
the pills
surging through my blood
the pot
fogging up my brain
I hope my death
is on a rainy day
but not this one

VI.

My fear of heights
has kept me off the highroad
and middle ground
is not my style
the scum of the earth
is always stuck to my shoes
just another addict
to look down on
from the safety of elevation
but I know how to rise
without the luxury of wings
and I know how to crash
without the safety of landing gear
so today you hover and shine
while my filthy habit
gets me messier still
but we all end up
under six feet of dirt

VII.

The captain
goes down with the ship
my rundown body
is the floundering
foundering
boat
battered violently
by the same waves
I used to ride for pleasure
each pill
is a pin prick
to my vessel
springing too many leaks
to patch
and manage
too many leaks
for two hands to handle
distress calls and life jackets
will not save me now
there is no time
left to buy
running out of the currency
most people call luck

VIII.

Here I am again
accelerating my life
head on
toward Death's Siren song
here I am once more
falling
through the doors
and smiling
because I'm not dead
testing the boundary of breath
sizing up Death
with a foot in my grave
we acknowledge and wave
we'll meet again soon
when I shoot for the moon
we'll meet again soon
like long lost friends
we'll meet again soon
the end of my end

IX.

Today I fished
off the end of a dock
and watched
a fat night crawler
at the top
of the heap
in my doomed little bucket
desperately digging down
trying to
escape the sun
he isn't even aware
of my hook
yet
it's the light he fears
I empathize
he has to wriggle around
and maneuver himself
through
shit and dirt
just to find a little
peace in the dark
I understand
I see my early death
my body
sinking into our
pillow top mattress
or sliding down
into a warm bubble bath
a night crawler
is stabbed repeatedly
nearly drowned
and then eaten alive
today my life
is a little prettier than usual
I granted amnesty
to my remaining slimy captives
and walked home
with a smile on my lips

X.

How could I
have been so
sculpted
and baked
like my life
had already
been hand carved
by hands
that are not mine?
I was completely
disappointed
as if
I was
completely done
but now
my face is cold
and busted
and grinning
organically
my ever
active hands
are rubbed raw
from the
reworking
of a life
no longer set
like a tombstone

Bekah Steimel

This One Thing I Pray

Truly I am
enamoured,
the very
idea so
appealingly
romantic
and final.

Darkest comfort.

I make it
grander in
my imaginings,
the way
a saddened
life-worn wife
of a more
stable man
might believe
excitement and
passion eternal
rests in a
drunken poet-

some prick
studying medicine
and on constant
look out
for a better option
than a crying
girl on the
kitchen floor

can't
compare at
first
to a dark
artist yearning
to brush aside
reality
and cry too.

Who is to say
it is not
the better choice?
Higher than
the mundane
and exceedingly
superior
to the unyielding
despair
that is my lot.

I am just
so tired and
too lazy
to carry
through, how?

I am not
a baker as
Plath,
so undignified.

As if I still
had pride,
traded
again to be sure

she was aware
I suffered.

The Holy
have quenched
my thirst
with vinegar,
a young priest
twists the tails
of Jonathan, David
and flees
that my sin
will not
befoul his pleasure.
He is Gods man.

How then?

Fire arms
seem iffy
and poisons
old school,
fancy flight
from building
or bridge?
luck has not
been kind,
too easily
then a crippled
ugly on the
surface
as my heart
has lived.

Sure I would

kiss death
and gamble
that there was
nothing
but darkness to
follow
but I am
a man of little
ambition
and drive.

It is no business
but mine
to make that choice
but I would
rather it blossomed
a surprise
as a blue-headed weed

yet soon

and my prayer
each night
to a god I hate
is to take me
and give me

this one thing
relief.

Justin Booth

Amnesia

The best side-effect
Of all the shit I did
Was to forget about it,
Not just the cost
All the actual and potential
Things I'd lost,
But those I'd got
That made me shake
That made me cough
Like sucking cock
Never did like it much
But did it more than once
In all those years of fun

The best side-effect
Of all the shit I did
Was to forget about it
When the plasticine savor
Of that fine crack flavor
Hit my bloodstream
Then my brain
That inhalation was better
Than mere oxygen
To hold the hit,
As long as I could
Bell-ringer, hum-dinger
Crying moment of clarity
White light from the mouth of infinity
Feeling like I'm one with divinity
Ten seconds... past its gone
Maybe thirty, if I was lucky
The rest of the trip, dirty and sucky

Not like licky, licky fucky fucky
More like carpet-crawling,
Searching and hiding
In closet by the front door
In the couch on the floor
Till we could get a grip
And go get some more

The best side-effect
Was to forget all about it
Night after night
Chasing that first hit
Till dawn's early light
Frantically trying to nap
Right before work
Then going on in,
Some bloodshot, insomniac jerk,
To do stuff so shitty
They let guys like me on board
I'd and shake and sweat
Just waiting for the moment
I could once again forget

The best side-effect
Of all the shit I did
Was that god-damned first hit
White light, sick shit
Heart in my chest
Beating like a fist
I gave everything I had for it
Just for the chance to forget

The best side-effect
Of all the things I've left
Was the taste

Of the river, Lethe
All the shit I did
Trying to forget about it
Lapping at the shores
Like a thirsty dog
Desperate for anesthesia
I woke up in the operation
IV cocaine in my veins
Made crack look like lollipops
Like being bent
Over a table and raped
By an infinite number
Of huge prison cocks

Somehow, then
I knew it had to stop
A loser weenie
Moving back in with Mommy
At the age of thirty
Was far better
Than the dirty slavery
I'd put upon me
No more coke for me
But beer and pot,
Pills, opiates, and ecstacy
Mushrooms and LSD
Well, you'll just have to see
That, as they say
Is another story

The best side-effect
Of all the shit I did
I'll never forget it
Clean at forty
With a beautiful wife

The sweetest woman
Who ever shared my life
Knows all about me
Still wants me
I have a career and
A humble home
With a mortgage on
Pets and moderate prosperity
Feeling like I'm one with divinity
Somehow being clean and sober
Seems to mean I don't do
The same shit over and over

Brad Wood

Monsters

I really want to talk about the sex
and about the drugs
more about the sex
the drugs
appear to be self-medicating symptoms
of my introduction to sex
which feels so good
but was begotten by monsters
that did not hide under the bed
but lied under the covers
with me
and the sex
now feels so good
like monsters
made friendly
like Hollywood
like I learned to like the monsters
like the drugs
like I learned to like the sex
with the monsters
like a drug
I want to talk about the monsters
I'm not supposed to like the monsters
but somehow
some part of me
identifies
the boy traumatized
confused
handed bedtime stories
by monsters
that didn't hide
under the bed

but spoke lies
too afraid to come out
from behind closets
bedtime stories
that spoke to the body
before the mind
said that sex was ok
some part of me
the boy
traumatized
identifies
with abandonment
into the loneliness
so much
that any hug will do
I want to talk about the sex
And the drugs
More about the sex
For I am predator
for the monsters
have trained me to be prey
and the monsters clutched my whispers
from the dark
I want to talk about the drugs
that hide
whatever actions
took place under their cloak
the drugs
that convinces
it all feels euphoric
the lack of drugs
and the increase amount of sex
and the lack of sex
and the increased amount of drugs
and how they seem to tie

into one another
meeting sometimes
at the right times
where there is just enough of both
to add to the confusion
and in my sober moments
I crave the monsters
more than the drugs
I want to talk about the monsters
I'm not supposed to like the monsters
I don't want
to talk about no more
about the sex
about the drugs
it was never about the sex
or about the drugs
it was always about
the monsters
it was always about
the monsters
it was always about
the monsters
It was always about
Me

Christoper Johnson

4:22 AM:
Tripping on K-Pins

23 Klonopin and a case of beer;
Still I talked the doctors into letting
Me go home.

Five hours later, I was roaming the streets;
Looking for a new Minotaur to battle...

I am a Bull-God...

Sorry Kid Rock...

You thought of the song—but I
was the inspiration.

Not even trying to kill myself
Can stop destination anywhere.

I defied death; went to the abyss,
In my sleeveless shirt
With no tattoos
With no Samaritans of mercy to sing to me...

Just an idea...a journey into
Arthur's Season in Hell...

I played sly tricks on madness too Rimbaud
But refused to say uncle when the
Fire got too hot...

Motifs are never simple when the
Rain and the wind last seven days and
Thirty two nights.

Staggering for a thought...
Apoplectic lethargy while tripping
on K-Pins...staggering through Worcester
via Painted Post
(Why do I think such thoughts?)

Knocking on bricks towards eternal love that
Pangs when I move the slightest degree to the
Left—because I want to be so good in spirit but
The combustible aftershock of a pleasant duration always...
                                        always leads me back
                                        to the mire.

I'm sick of walking in the muck alone...
Tired of crisis and despair—a wanton creature
Of forced defiance.

A slave of misdeeds I thought were true...just a
Minute in the sphere of existence...

We are all that (stuck); despite what she thinks, or
He thinks or I think...

Games are for fools who never get to live twice.

Only one chance at the precious.

Never two opportunities
Only one...
One time
        For clarity...

Dan Provost

How to watch me wither

Sit on winter's lap.
Drink from the fountain of death.
Color the walls in mold.
Take a selfie at a funeral.

Sand bathe.
Yell out obscenities to the moon.
Be fair and tell the sun its worth.

Drink tequila with a straw.
Read a poem to a mute parrot.
 Grab a nopal by the throat.

Light up a cigarette from the wrong end.
Form a single file line.

Point and shoot.

lift me up again,
don't give me water

inject me with sour milk
and hobo urine

take away my books
and let me cry on the skin
of dead trees.

Edward Vidaurre

May.

Time spins out like
a top encountering
a crack in the sidewalk,
loops drunkenly into summer.

There is nothing finer than
my lady's deep pink
fingernails, nothing finer
than her blood-plump lips,
ripe-red as the robin's breast
as he flits and picks insects on our lawn.

I've come so far from the moment
a monster cradled my heart like
a hand grenade, slid out
the pin with magazine teeth
and held me close for the last 3.2 seconds
of my uninterrupted sweetness.

Shrapnel used to surface from
my skin every time I
came but I am clean now,
lush and greener than ever.

I have finally learned to give more
than petty tokens – a pair of my underwear,
a few hand-written notes – more than things
to remember me by.

Logen Cure

Night Roaming.

Standing in the shadows, I see nothing
in my way
I long for a touch, some warm embrace
When I awake in the morning, as I
am surely asleep despite my lively
appearance,
will I be aware of anyone's admiration
other than my own?
Night turns to day and turns to night
again, still I am here where I always am

If only for one night, I could feel...
anything
So alone, yet cloaked in the armor of
imaginary friends
Convinced of grandeur, talented as Poe.
Or Frost.
Perhaps.
Here in the light where nobody lives.
Here in the dark where hope dies.

The town is mine.
I walk the path so trodden in the
sunlight, yet unmolested at this hour.
The dirty laundry of my past behind me,
a crying child is alive in the void.
I seek inspiration from The Poet, the
approval of the only one I see as greater
than myself.

His voice is mine, I tell myself. I am as
gifted as he.

His words inspire and touch hearts.
My words die before they ever reach computer screen or yellow lined paper.
Here with my only friend, I walk the streets alone, and pontificate boldly in my mind.

Me, Myself, and I, the only crowd I incite. Grand conversation and debate with no one. The poison liquid is warm and surprises me with thoughts of my own demise.
Would I be better off? Would you?
It would be weeks before anyone was aware.

The Poet said that a life unlived is worse than dying but that is wrong.
As long as I am alive, I am the victor.
If only for words I could live a life of solitude.
"Be careful what you wish for" fills my mind.

Like the unreachable love that was never there, I am an illusion.
Words flow from her mouth, so you know these are lies.
Will I ever get past my failure?
The ultimate failure, I feel.
Gave my life to a fantasy, to a dream. Like everything else I loved and believed in, false.

The well-meaning voices imply that there is a brighter day.
There isn't.
Rearing it's ugly head, the once forgotten insistence upon guilt;
Upon reconciliation.
Free of guilt, for I have done no wrong. Yet everything is a result of my choices.
Could there have been intent?
Self hatred hides like forbidden love.
Is it only in the dark I know myself?

Eric Blackerby

Coming Early

Fort Worth Summer of 2011

It's been so hot I had a dream the trees were leaving and then the fires came.
                              —random conversation overheard at local grocery store
He said his name was Chick or Chin or Chin the Mango Juice.
                              —passerby
No one is asking what happened to all the homeless. No one cares, because it's easier to get on the subway and not be accosted.
                              —Richard Linklater

I melt
Like some forgotten cup
Balancing hot-cold & alone
On a shrinking patch of shade

Behind the drug store
Under a parapet of brick
Holding the thesaurus I use as a pillow
Or a note from friends

Are you listening
It was a time
Of soiled bedrolls and empty parking space
Lemon-yellow lines and dreams of falling

Showering in a handsink
Four feet off the floor
Praying for an allowance
Of common soap and uncommon privacy

The sound of movement in the morning
Steering wheels—tires humming

Sour bodies and sweet gasoline
Pulling in on itself like urban origami

Chin The Mango Juice
Remembers rest
In the common verity of repose
Like an absent limb finding a missing itch

Dry-heart
Dry-eye
Dry-well
I have not the words for this

The assistant drug store manager
In her garden takes notice and approaches
To shake me off the small comfort
Of a wee dark spot oozing need like molasses

Why are you lying down

The blacktop
Is hot & glassy on my back
Pulling against the buttercup growing in my chest
Our breath goes up and down

The ground like a lid
Opening and closing
And the rising heat
Saturates the spirits so

Foreign & close
I hearLove-songs/Mad-songs
To the apparitions
And the Heat

IhaveBurned dead grass for body hair
Teeth are clouds and the wind
Blowing through them hurts
I like stacks of ripping things

Dirty wings
Pull missing teeth
Lap-dance for me
Sweat is a wound and an ocean of stank

I am sweat
I am my life
A wreck erected
Behind the Diamond Sham Rock

I am in leagueWith dripping things
Chalk dust copsErasers cleaned
Cotton mouth/Liquor store
Wine in the forest/Forest in the door

Sun in a ditchOff the edge
Of a dick-dead shadelessParking lot
The color of a gun
Pink like love and my dry tongue

From the kisk of scissors
To the nailing lid
Pick the homegrown buttercup
Lick the emptydumpsterbuttercup

And hold something like the sun

Paul Koniecki

Summers

On days that the unit
would chug and hum
in a battle against
mid-day heat it's
valor no equal to ability.

We would wake long
before we wanted and
we would fix knowing
that would mean an extra
one to cop that night.

Sometimes there would
still be a bottle and
we would drink brown
from the plastic cups
that came with clean towels,
from Flo's cart.

It was the closest we came,
ever, to being us. People.
To having conversations,
the regular kind or
at least how we imagined.

I told her I wished I loved her.

She asked if I knew
any games that didn't feature death.

Justin Booth

Cripple

I remember the first day
I woke up with a paralyzed brain.
The bed was my prison.
Sleep was my savior.
I wasn't ready to face the world,
Wasn't heart-headed, open, toes curled
I used to want to be seen,
But all I wanted in that moment was a glowing screen
That showed the person I used to be.
Looking in the mirror, I could see past me
Every few days, the same song on repeat
"What's wrong?"
Nothing.
"What's wrong?"
Nothing.
If I told you I know you wouldn't believe it.
I've become a Cerebral quadriplegic.
See-through suffering from invisible bleeding,
The sore ache of the give-a-fuck that keeps on leaving.
Wasting whole days drenched in a mental fog
The textbook definition of backlogged.
Comforting myself with visions of removing this flawed, fickle fiend from the world,
But I never come fully unfurled.
I'm a survivor not because of any one event,
But because of a collected experience.
I battle an invisible illness affecting 1 in 4 people in the United States.
Every day that I wake up and take on the world is a tiny victory.
I fight for those who fight with me.
Not just friends and family,
But so many others who get just as paralyzed as me.
Your morning may break you, but you've got to believe
That every day you wake and breathe
Is a day closer to getting your brain back on its feet.

Helen Coy-Gresavage

It

You see through it, live in it, cry about it...but you can never describe it until the painting is dry or blood is running out of your mouth, It becomes a penance, a misnomer of daily functioning...death-life, life-death...cut the crow beat the dust run until your next landing stop minus man. Light is not to stare at or go into...It is to leave as fast as you can.....it, it, it, it, becomes a forfeit of life dark and death light. Crows fly away from it, paths point arrows to which way to go....songs sung by forlorn acoustic guitar players....it is the smell of tears it is the waste of talent, the discarding of fascination by young angelic boys who told too many lies while doing it in the bathroom...mental masturbation is so starry physical whacking-off is just exercise. The lonely fold their arms, contemplate death's tomorrow and watch for it in the back room of jaded killers and peasant queens.

The linear explosion has passed only it remains....hers it is the son that never came back from war, his is the wife that left for his best friend—it is the fear and angst I feel when rising out of bed. Songs sung from some long ago southern rock group let me escape it for a minute or two—but the horror, the stifled screams, the list of commas that concern it. It, it ,it never escapes, never runs, never tries to make friends with you...it just sits there, eating at your soul...corroding your arteries until breath is impossible...Yes it....I know you and I fear you...I hate you and do not understand you. Poor mothers who sons who died, yours is pure evil while my mind takes a more slow, diabolical approach. So I live on...within it...the death part is pure slow insanity while the living establishes itself despite the urge for the knife, the gun or the pills. Why do I feel this way? The tint of the sun shines on afternoon despair—1:35 PM, we are all in escape mode from it at this hour. Sad; slip away from the mindset...no shiny happy people perfect... walk alone bloated with agony. I am not manipulative... just waiting for the end of the day...it happens....it happens...

Dan Provost

Ode To Tortured Artist.

Ah, you tortured artist,
when will you learn?
You snap the whip across your own back,
and wait for the burn.
The massive blurring twisted hungry world tortures you.
Infinity, and all of its transgressions,
throughout and without time immemorial, tortures you.
The page you raped with your seed of ink,
the white forever spoiled for demented thoughts
you cannot contain; this tortures you.
People, loud, opinionated, selfish, swarming, fighting,
fucking, birthing, dying all in vain, they torture you!
And to write! Oh the indignities to be suffered!
The therapy sessions you should have had when instead,
you turned like an addict to that dusty composition notebook; you
are sick!
You are suffering!
You need help!
And still, no intervention, goddammit no, let me wallow in the filth
of my prison,
twisting, producing angelic cries from demonic contortions;
the ground is soaked with dirty blood—why won't you die?!
The drunken madness of it all, a plethora of pills and orgies, alcohol
and the occasional herb.
Healing my ass, you're just looking to escape and get high.
Meanwhile, excuse me, pardon me, but do you have a minute?
I seem to have written this, and why should you care?
Like a street minister peddling tracts of biased salvation to those
they deem 'lost,'
you wander thru life, leaving behind pages and pages of no gospel,
no savior, no salvation, and no devil or god but yourself to exorcise;
and leave it in rhyme so the demons can dance to it!

And where was my mind?

Off in my own head composing sonnets to stars and sunrises, angry letters to god and family, and ultimatums to facaded friends.

You're stuck there now, aren't you?

Trapped inside your own head, either screaming to be let out, the horrors are too great!

Or getting comfy in the dark extra space your mind dares no longer occupy, like a tenet fearing the crazy man at the end of the hall.

(I hear screams and music emanating from that room at night! I think he's an eccentric rapist or killer savant!)

For God's sake man!

Your head is not a room with a view in an upstairs apartment with a pissed off landlord and a shitty fall-apart building!

You can't live there if you already inhabit the space!

Oh tortured soul, your poems to suicide go unheeded by their muse.

I told you before man, she's busy in California, she WILL NOT fuck you!

You don't own a gun or even enough willpower to stick your dick in her and fuck yourself into oblivion.

The ride that goes nowhere has the highest fee, the longest line, and the most twisted fucking operator.

Abyss is not your funhouse, artist, pay your toll and get out!

I am my own whipping boy!

I misbehave, I must be punished.

My body fails, it should rot today!

I have no effort, I don't contribute,

just grab that knife and bleed out your sins,

you walking cesspool of sickening brilliance and raw emotion!

Grow a pair, meet a girl, (or a boy,) and let them punish you!

The works that come forth hence will be wonderful and brilliant by design,

and miserable line by agonized line.

Pour me a drink, and share your stage.

I have a song to sing.

Ode To Fuck All!

Fuck the bawdy crowds!

Fuck the rotten children!
Fuck the dream and nightmare!
Fuck the waking world!
Fuck the fly and hornet!
Fuck your judgment.
Fuck reincarnation. (Shit returns as more shit.)
Fuck this interruption!
Fuck the cosmic scale of balance!
Fuck the coward fathers!
Fuck death and fuck returning!
Fuck all,
Fuck off,
Fuck me,
Fuck yourselves!
The torture is weighty and delicious and palpable and otherworldly.
He must be so brooding!
The depth is beautiful but deadly to experience.
Take your razor-blade poetry, get out,
take your indoctrination, I am the dragon and the pit,
there will be no soliciting here, loitering is permitted by the
talented only who have proven themselves, and otherwise,
on rainy Thursdays in June by all else,
take your mouth, place it here, pay the fee,
bend over, grit and grin, take it like a woman, man,
and go!
The bard has wept,
the drunk has slept in,
the pen is vomiting in an alley.
My pain is my bride, and she's always on the rag,
you are the rag, soak it up!
Day in, day out,
inspiration, motivation,
desperation, lamentation,
mix them and swallow.
Take this pill,

don't ever call me,
go home and bleed on a canvas,
you tortured soul,
despicable artist,
loathsome writer,
worthless drunk,
hopeless addict,
clueless poet.
Take your art and eat it,
throw up on an accomplished writer's shoe,
and really get it all in there!
Tell him that's poetry, you sold out dick,
and move on.
But please don't stop the torture, god, man, people, self,
heroes, mind, heart, body.
Damn all love, the source of pain,
dip in the well,
write until your fingers bleed,
bleed until you're weak,
sleep it off, wake up,
get fucked, write drunk.
Torture me now God, as you see fit,
because for fuck's sake, my poetry still sucks,
and I must not be doing it right...

James Barrett Rodehaver

Whiskey Psalm.

Whiskey and I are quiet lovers,
seldom do we find ourselves dancing,
we were gods kissing nights away in our twenties,
staggering silly,
I've been writing love letters to empty bottles for ten years
now,
getting thirsty, belly empty-heart hollowed
learning to love the way winter feels in my nostrils,
passion sugared our skin raw,
satisfying, comfortable,
I am afraid the ghosts we were will claw back into the
threshold of my palms,
splitting maps built with experience,
breaking me in a caress like a stolen rosary.

Jennifer E. Hudgens

I'll be out in a minute.

There were 83 of them—
pills like reasons like excuses—
lined up little opportunities

to feel
less.

The bathroom lights made a pattern
of bright reflections on the counter –

and I couldn't look at the mirror

because it
has always
lied.

I had line upon line
uneven in one place (odd numbers)
and I could see 16 being less than infinity—

I could see 16 being the endpoint of a very short number
line—

I could see
sixteen and eighty-three
and the infinite tiny moments,
every blink and breath and thought
between zero
and now.

I envisioned eighty-three swallows
and wondered how many minutes it would take

to be done.

And then I remembered
the infinite words I'd never gotten around to saying
and thought that I couldn't fit them all

into a suicide note.

I remember eighty-three sounds of pills falling back into
their container
and sixteen reasons to walk out of the bathroom
and no less than infinite reasons
to live.

Logen Cure

NYD... WNYL?

This thing in my head?
Might as well be cancer, it's post-trautmatic stressful death,
a thousand voices, all of them sounding like screeching gackles
hanging in the trees outside in early dusk,
their white-noise cackles
drive me nuts.
That's exactly how this mood disorder goes in me,
some psychological,
concentration cramp
that concencrate me
in neverending migraines,
turning sunshine and joy into endless pain and rains,
but I often wonder how many times
an icepick to the temple would deliver me
from this insanity...
dual lobes screaming some melodramatic symphony
as directed by a Norwegian death metal band
all dragging anchor chains and rusty hooks screeching
across metal floors...
it's enough
to make a man choke himself
with his own goddamn hand.

So, I take this pharmaceutical relief...
this bullet (*in the form of a drug) slowly killing me.
rather than exploding my brain, blood and skull
It implodes my emotions,
turning me ever inward and makes my world that
more grey and dull.
Might as well be incurable?
Who am I?
Does it really matter?

In a world of paragraphs
held in such high statute,
I am a just a dusty, $1.00 Half-Price marked,
dogearred and yellowed well-worn parable.
If the world is full of number "ones" and "zeroes,"
I am barely a decimal.
This disease has weakened me...
it has acted beligerently,
ruthlessly,
callously,
viciously,
ambitiously,
carelessly,
sadistically....
sorry, my story has turned into
an unplanned party of three....
me, myself and my pity.

After hoping that a million papercuts from this poem
drown me in a sea of crimson,
I wake up from my stupor and lay my emotions to rest, post mortem
and walk to the edge of the short pier, then off it into that sea
of self derision,
and float on it, this dead sea of dead thoughts. I breathe deep
knowing that I will not die. Not for a second.
...Not that I'm too much of a coward to die....
but that I'm too much a bastard, who wants to live
long enough to prove
those noises
wrong.

So I swallow my pill
in this shitty apartment...
take a long, deliberate puff
from my Black & Mild...

letting the smoke filter in and out
like a metaphysical
highway to
dimensions in my soul that have yet
to be defined....
sip my cognac from my plastic Disney "Jungle Book" glass....
and figure that if I have been
given
the gift of
being not dead yet...
why not yet live ?

Coyote Wiley

Recidivists

Does it make you feel noble,
There at the bar, with all the other
White-collared, white-washed, conspiratorial smiles?
Do you feel pride and purpose?
Was law school worth it,
Serving up penal punishment like cold, bologna sandwiches?
Are you content in the evening, with justice and Jesus?

 Or, is it just a job to you?

I've been here before
Shit,
Not free for 60 days
Already back to my criminal ways.
We keep shooting the same scene,
Playing the same roles,
Using the same script,
Slamming those same doors.

Statistically, I knew I'd be back again.
And that you'd still sit there, with that same white-bread grin.

Your prison worked so well the first time,
Ferguson Unit, red-bricked, dog-pound
What could be different, this time down?
Dominguez Unit, State Jail-bound.
16 months to wonder how.
RECIDIVIST—State Pen
Texas, ape-shit, off the deep end.

What about that coveted "accountability?"
Christian pick-up truck, judges and juries?

What a waste, if you never "reformed" me.

Rehabilitation went out (when)
The needle came back (in)
Redemption contingent on a background check
Is it any wonder that there is no respect in me left
For all you hold sacred, for all you believe
When all it ever came down to, was double-fuck ME?

Fuck YOU!
Find something new.
What can you do when the truth
No longer proves true?

As I sign my plea, we see the same thing
Recidivists, slithering back here again

So, I'll sign on the line.
I'll retreat in my mind,
To the terrible places that you'll never find
   (until the next time)
When, we will gather together, with roles well rehearsed
You'll know my lines, and I'll know yours.

Recidivists.

PW Covington

Unopened Letter

Dear Mom,
You once asked me what I wanted...and...
I want to go one day without crying.
I want to be able to plant seeds of decisions
And it not sprout apples of apprehension
Or oranges of origamic reasons,
Folding one over the other, again and again
Into a thousand beautiful mistakes
Resembling swans and flowers but not sound judgment.
For once, I want love to stop by and just say hey
And only if invited in, will come bearing gifts and upon departure,
Leave empty handed and both of us on good terms.
I want my memories to remember me
When they tie me up with their mental masochism
When I make mention I'm not into S&M
So my tears are not whips but seeds and
I want to be able to plant seeds of decisions
And it not sprout apples of apprehension and
Oranges of origa...

...I want to stop having to go through the same stuff over and over again.

I want my family and friends to tell me they believe in me,
But with their backs turned so I can't see what their eyes are really saying
And they can't see mine well up with water because they know the truth.
I want to go one day without crying.

I want to write like Poe, dance like Astaire,
Sing like Ella, act like Denzel,
I want to laugh like Q, make people laugh like Bluz,
I want to preach like Elder Grant and teach like Pastor Greg.
I want to love like a 3 year old,

Learn the arrogance of a cat
And the loyalty of a golden retriever.
I want to look at life and not get an attitude.
Mama, I just want to make...you...happy.

By the time you read this... I'll be dead.

So now I guess I can add your happiness to the list of things
I won't accomplish because of this.
And I know you believe I'll go to hell for this
But don't worry, Mama, it's cool...
I'm just being transferred.

Sorrow has been sitting in my soul so long,
It's started to charge ME rent and
I just don't have the emotional capital
So I'm gonna move out before I'm evicted.
And suicides go to hell?
There's no justice in that!
What's the sin in giving in?
I was only destined to burn in heaven forever
If I continued to live the comfortable lie of litanies locked away
To which the only keys were on my knees
And how many times do I have to hear "no"
Before I know this life isn't for me.

Let not your disappointment wax long, mama,
As if YOU did something wrong.
Pick the blame up from your feet,
Put it in the urn with my ashes,
Turn it into mud with your tears and
Place it into God's hands
And maybe He'll make a better me next time.

Maybe He'll lessen the talent and add more common sense.
Tweak my trust mechanism so it doesn't expel so much.
Fix the crack in my head gasket,
Replace the shocks in my heart.
Drano my pipes so His Spirit, as water,
Will flow more freely through me.
Download a doubt protector.
Install Norton Antivirus and a wireless connection
So answers to prayers will come clearer and without interruption.
This may take a while, Mama.

I'm a complicated anomaly.

So maybe the new me will learn from my mistakes.
Don't you get it, Mama, I'm not killing myself.

I'm just giving God a clean slate.

Tavis P. Brunson

My Demon

It came in the form
of an invisible wind
that seized me off
my feet, held every
muscle paralyzed,
scratched out
my right eye,
then cut off slips of
my tongue—tiny slivers,
left me terrorized.
When would it come again?
I levitate above my bed,
light as a feather,
stiff as a board,
clutching the Ouija—
Looking, searching
for my demon again
until I find it and
ask it why me and
it attacks me in the form
of smothering blankets,
cologne, heat,
vomit—an irresistible
urge to die.

Trier Ward

Ode to Cut

Reinvent me. Cut.
There are hiding
places. On a
railroad overpass looking
at the moon.
This night needs
saving. Cut. This
night needs proof.
Cut. Everything needs
saving, perspicacity, and
proof. Make her
a short brunette.
Make her a
sideways gouger. Make
her a suspension
bridge. Make her
gravity. Like the
beating of a
devil's heart make
her in tune.
They taught us
the world turns
away from the
sun. Set down
your broken promises.
The darkness is
my blood. Balancing
on the edge
of an overpass,
cutting the letters
'perilous', a long-lost
acrobat wonderful and

hemorrhaging, I can
taste it in
my ruin. The
folly of my dermis
must be set
free. Tonight I
am your diver.
Tonight I am
your champion. Tonight
I'm going downtown
and bleed for
your escape. White
Eye. Pale Disk.
Circumnavigator. Lost Twin.
Help. Cut Me.
Make her a
flagon of smoke.
Make her a
switchblade memory. Make
her a forgotten
bell. Du Bist
Salvador. The clocks
in your eyes
melt and burn
and tick beneath
my skin. Tethered.
Mooring. I can
feel you. Cut.
You slit me.
Cut. To learn
to manage pain,
Bright Falangist, Anemic
Circle in the
sky, bring knives.
Bring words like

blood. Bring blades
like nothing. More
than a jumper
on a bridge
means to the
blotter. Pre Exilic
Prophet. Post Exilic
Corpse. More than
the sharpest edge
of night means
to the moon.

Paul Koniecki

#phoenix

At the pinnacle of survivor spirit, the phoenix represents rebirth, and renewal. Everyone survives in their own way. When we celebrate what we have survived, and who we've become as a result of our transformative experiences, we realize how blessed we are, because we are Not Dead Yet!

Photo by Chuck Taylor

Travelmarvel

I haven't always been silent.

I used to sing
and tell tales.

Now I'm
absent, distant, elsewhere.

(Ensconced among
deepwhile cushions.)

(The shock of loss
but in fact gain.)

Now I'm
changing, dark-adapted.

Now I'm
pacing and replacing,

now I'm
twink-attracting forces.

Then with fresh, unblinking eyes
I give final,
sensuous
contours to the light.

The infiltrated solange.

Then I might talk,
proud,
untouchable.

Agnes Marton

Jericho A.D.

just because
we're outsiders,
don't think we can't see in.
you might as well
be swimming around
in an aquarium,
so caught up in
your microcosm,
you can't see past
your bulletproof glass
that's just about to come caving in,
leaving you flopping around
gasping for air
in a world full of streetwise kats
closing in.
who's downsized now?
who's less apt to survive?
we've been hard-knock schooled
on methods of creative survival,
and we're the ones
who bore your burdens on our backs
allowing you to thrive.

we're outsiders,
by chance or by choice,
but just because you're tone deaf,
you think we have no voice.
you've forgotten the story
of Joshua and Jericho
both history and allegory—
the cracks are starting to show.
chants and songs, rants and slams,

internet and pens in hand;
knock one of us down, ten step in,
dire multiplications you can't spin.

just because we're outsiders,
we don't fit into your graphs;
forged in the fires of God
for purposes you can't grasp.
the implications are more than historical,
they're practically paleontological:
when the dinosaurs,
the giants of old, began to stumble,
it was the small, meek creatures—
preyed on, stepped on, or ignored—
that survived simply because
they were humble,
now grown into a throng!
can't you hear the rumble?
can't you hear the song?
it's the march of thousands of thousands
footsteps, the chants of thousands of
thousands of voices denied,
setting of tremors as they advance.

your tower of Babel is caving in,
your cruise ship is about to capsize,
your party's due for a monumental crash;
too late, you've finally realized
that your new Jericho's about to be downsized
by the outsiders
who've lived too long outside your walls.

Todd "Grendel" Pack

The Phoenix

Beaten, strangled and abused,
She thought the darkness would consume her.

She hung her head low and hid deep inside her soul.
"You can't run and you can't hide," her enemies taunted.

The light, so bright pushed through her mind.
She lifted her eyes and stared deep into the darkness.
Fear, destruction, hate
She wasn't going to let them destroy her.

She pushed past the pain,
Broke her chains free,
And entered into the heart of darkness.

Battle by battle,
The demons held her down and defeated her.
She struggled until she could take no more.
She fell to the ground with only hope to guide her.

The demons cheered then grew still.
The cavern of her personal hell trembled.
Out of her ashes arose with the flames of fire the most beautiful creature.
A fiery angel with flames the never burned her with the face of their victim.

One by one, she killed all her demons.
She flew out of the darkness with her eyes on the sky.
Higher and higher she flies with a strong spirit, clean soul and love in her heart.

Born out of her struggles into a strong creature.
Her past no longer defines her.

Allison Bruning

Untitled

I am broken Water
believing out loud
at the eternal church
of bad singing
where the snake mouth orchard grows
Me
Corner crouched
Instagram freak
Social media monk
Music movement
Chair dancer
Me
Magi
Asian waist grinder voyeur
Not so shy quiet guy
Me
Rhythm slave
Venus Sub
Direct experiential slut

Sun sign dominate
Cape Verdean woman baby daddy
Me
Mixed Magic Black Rep
Nuyorican Brooklyn Moon
Progeny
What you know about this Ju Ju?
I lay mountains to sand
Stretch rivers
To ocean sized bed sheet puddles
What you know about me?
1200 techniques to serrato
Digital dance floor

Headphone silence loneliness
No roof over my trees
Do you think you know me?
Some say I talk to much
In actuality
I say nothing
Use sound to tweak perception
Outsiders peering in
Always guessing
Me
Soul rhythm and blues funk
Me
Country rock and roll metal
Me
Afro beats Jazz blues house disco
and whatever you call Barry Manilow
You don't know me
Sexual assault survivor
Suicide attempt survivor
Single parent mother survivor
I'm flashing back

To past divine

Vertebrae star shine

Adolescence innocence

 Untouchable confidence

Teenage magnificence

Strike twice lightening

I need you right now

First generation Jim crow refugee survivor

Inner city crack epidemic survivor
Desert Storm survivor
Manic Depression Survivor
Magellan the philosophy of felons

 Mental criminal

Ice pick master locs

Dreaded Moor Prince

Vagina twitch bewitched

Even if

Only for a second

Catholic school boy in brick city survivor
Texas department of corrections survivor
Black on black crime survivor
Black man in America survivor
Where did that kid go

Fearless in the mirror

I search for him now

All I see is a hollow appearance

You know nothing about me.
You only know what you heard
Read
Or as seen on tv
But you don't know
Me

Christopher Johnson

They Sicken

"They sicken of the calm who know the storm."
             - Dorothy Parker

They sicken of the calm
who know the storm,
it holds no promise.

The calm is a
black hole sucking
life in.

The storm is Life,
twisting, screaming
and dancing near Death.

Once you have
counted coup on
codeine and car wrecks,

been shot at and missed
every good thing
seems mundane.

Reality stands no chance
when sharpened point imaginings
soar infinitely.

The coolest green grass
of contentment is no memory
compared to swimming
the crashing surf of melancholy.

Those who know the storm
cringe against days blinding rays
but are comforted at the breast
of darkest night.

Justin Booth

Like a Fox

mere intelligence is overrated,
experts are dumbfounded,
officials are astounded,
and off to one side in the high grass,
someone laughs.

it's that ten-spot you found tucked
in your pocket
when you thought you were broke.

it's something standing next to the
streetlight
that doesn't cast it's own shadow.

it's a quick trip, a zipline into a cool pond,
the way those street-kids displaced into
the forest
laugh and applaud the first time
you ride it down and let go,
silly legs flailing.

"where are you going?
where are you going?"
where i'm going, and where
i'll know when i get there . . .
but you won't.

it's a glimmer in the raingutter
dismissed by passers-by as a bit of tinfoil
that's actually a two-headed quarter,
almost a month's worth of lucky days
if you pick it up.

it's a slanting light at sunset
that shows you something
you lost a long time ago,
so long ago
that you never missed it.

it's tearing open an adversity
like a rascally rabbit,
finding a tasty treasure of wisdom.

"it must be a disease.
it must be something like rabies.
it must be shot . . ."
but you couldn't find the magic bullet
in a thousand-and-one tales,
and i'll be sitting at your dinner table,
and while you're busy with debates
i'll steal the steaks right off your plates,
and pay you back with a smile.

"he's crazy."
my fourth-grade teacher said so.
my youth minister said so
(but with a twinkle in her eye).
"he's crazy."
the kids i ran with said so,
and all along they thought
i was running from them . . .
but it was the other way around.
this time, the fox chases the hounds.
"he's sick, he's insane, he's bipolar,
he's . . ."
crazy.

and now you know.
or you think you do.
tomorrow night's twilight edge
hasn't even been breached,
and i'm already planning for it,
Groucho spreading out blueprints.
for a house in which
he intends to search for a missing painting.

flip a coin, and i'll snatch it
before it lands in the dust.
pick a card, any card;
i've already stacked the deck.
mourn in the ruins,
i've already salvaged
from the wreckage
the jewels you rejected.

it's crazy to run like this,
when the fox has gray hairs in his pelt,
but his eyes still burn,
crazy-sly, funny-sad eyes
that i'm told betray
my emotions . . .
or maybe that's just what
i want you to think.

keep guessing, keep doubting,
because i'm still betting
i'll reach my destination
on this crazy-quilt path
that nobody but a lunatic would follow . . .
the necessity of my lunacy
won't let me hold back,
firmly in the grip of my destiny

and, paradoxically, inescapably free.

"you'll never get there.
it's not on the map.
you've got no GPS.
you've got no app.
you're crazy . . ."

oh, yes.
ask my cousins, they knew it long ago.
and as to your traps, i stole the bait
before you even set them,
and snatched your half-baked ideas
while they were cooling in the open
window.

just watch me run, and play, and fight,
and laugh all the long day and night
like a fox in the tall grass.

Todd "Grendel" Pack

Name

My name,
a gift to me from my father on my birthday,
a battle cry for his
sugary, spicey, victorious dark haired beauty.

Slick Colorado ice changed my name to FIRST SCAR.
Daddy held the gash closed
so they could stitch me a
permanent mark across my forehead.

In kindergarten, my name became GHOST
when I learned to hide.
I placed secret names on invisible love notes
safety-pinned to the valentine inside my chest.
This hurt.

I grew up
and fell in love with the little pistons
of a bright yellow Spitfire.
They changed my name to WIND and ROAD
and RAGE OF MY STEREO.

David changed my name to US,
then to FOREVER,
then to the blue sound of black FEAR.
When he changed my name to BITCH,
I had trouble answering.

I secretly called myself FORGIVER.

When my children changed my name to MOM,
I danced in such busy circles

that I almost forgot that
I'd ever had another name—
for years.

Divorce gave me back my father's name,
but it was loneliness
that changed my name to POET
and called me ARTIST.

Although I'd had many names,
Brian wouldn't call me by any of them.

One fool even tried to rename me
something "pretty" that he liked better.
This made me laugh.

My names have been
spoken,
bellowed,
whispered,
wept
and written.

I like to be called LOVE.
I answer to SECOND CHANCES,
but what I name myself
is that gift from may father
on my birthday.
I call myself
VICTORY.

D. Victory

Doppler Dreams

In that swirling mass
Of oscillating chaos
The moment before
The vertex crashes
Your universe is exposed
Fragile
Bone brittle
Disintegrating
Eclipsed in colours
Of lightening brightness
Fracturing the elliptic paths
Between thought and memory
And your planets shift
And your universes sway
To cerebral echoes
Crowned by orbed discords
In symphonies of silences
From each fissure
On every spiraled nebula
Across entire hemispheres
In those inter-cranial spaces
Of your inter-stella existence
In the dark grey matter
Beyond the known void...
Then gravity grips you
And the eyes flutter
Each star's shutter
On a flickering solar flare
Jerking your synaptic galaxies
Back, into life...

Emma van Woerkom

It's Gonna Hurt.

oh, you're damn right it's gonna hurt,
and when they wrap it, there will be an uncomfortable tightness around the wound.
you'll have to get up and walk before you think you're ready.
you'll have to take the stairs, as the wound throbs and complains under your sock.
you've been in bed long enough, and i know you won't like this.
the sun will be too bright, the shoe won't feel right,
and the pain will bite until you win.
you cannot give in, there's too much at stake.
if you lie there all day, you won't get any better.
keep walking, every day, keep trying.
are you gonna let your pain win?
don't let your body tell you what to do.
fight!
see this scar?
every bone, every tendon, every muscle was crying out,
the heart surgery had hurt worse than anything i've ever experienced.
but i was not going to lie there and pee in a cup every day, even though i wanted to.
i crawled, hands and knees raw, body screaming,
just barely inching my way to my "handi-capable" toilet,
and i stopped here and there to catch my breath and relax,
but i didn't stop until i could pull myself up onto the toilet,
with everything in me screaming in agony,
because even something as insignificant as a piss was worth trying for.
so stop complaining,
get up,
and walk down those stairs,
and across the parking lot,
and then turn around and walk to me,
all the way back across,
back to me,
because i'll be damned if i let you give up.
see this scar?

i stood in agony at the altar for 45 minutes straight to get married, a
month after my hip replacement,
because it was worth it, and i loved her.
i was happy.
i didn't lean,
i didn't wince,
i didn't cry.
i knew i could do it.
because i was up walking just days after the surgery,
and just a week later, despite the pain,
i sat her fat ass on the sink in the rehab hospital bathroom, and
fucked her, because i could!
because i wanted to.
it hurt like hell, but i can say i did it.
see these scars?
two different surgeries on my feet still didn't repair the damage done
by the bone disease.
it's a miracle i can still walk.
they hurt like hell, but every step spat in the face of my doctors.
i've had to re-learn to walk at least 4 times, and that's not counting
the first time i ever learned.
i just kept coming, no matter the pain.
today, they're so ugly and tender, i don't let most people even see
them,
let alone touch them.
i didn't even let my feet give up on walking, and they had given up.
i even dance, pain or no, because i can, and i might dance better than
you.
i wanted to give up a lot, but something in me won't let me, so i
don't.
now i won't ever stop trying.
so yes, it's gonna hurt,
you're gonna cry,
it's gonna suck balls,
but you are not going to LIE THERE AND GIVE UP!

walk, motherfucker!
you're a badass motherfucker!
i hurt every goddamn day due to a bone disease that's always
getting worse.
i tell myself that i'm a badass motherfucker, and i get up anyway.
it's gonna hurt,
but my friend,
giving up hurts worse.
i know you can do it,
because i'm nary 100 pounds,
and i'm a goddamn viking,
a tough-ass survivor poet,
a warrior fighting his disease every day, and winning,
a black-belt fighter of every fucking thing god throws at me,
and he does it because he knows i can do it!
so get up,
shut up,
and prove me right,
because if i can do it,
i know you can do it!!!

James Barrett Rodehaver

Twist

wither in the wind of these words,
and dither no more.
the tatters that rattle in this wind
are all that are left
of the warp and weft
of your pallid schemes.

 i say "no more."
i'm tired of holding my breath,
biting my tongue to shreds,
seething in silence
(doing my ragged digestive system
not a bit of good, to say nothing
of the strain on my already
damaged brain).

well, own your part of the damages,
because when you beat people over the head
with big, stupid things,
brain damage is kinda inevitable.

i'm starting to wonder
if there's much of a gap
between spiritual tyrants
and their financial and political
counterparts.

it's a gap that's rapidly closing,
and it takes an idiot not to notice it,
and that's just what you want:
a nation of idiots.
a totally apathetic population

that you can manipulate at will,
feeding them the swill
that "trickles down"
from your impacted bowels,
and using every technomantic
trick in the book
to look through our lives
like a library book (which also means
what library books
we're looking at).

and this is ACCEPTED.
and this is the NORM.
and this is so wrong . . . .

i say "no more."
because if Oliver Twist
had to eat shit like this,
he'd never have gotten
back in line,
and you herd us through
the malls that are stalls
training us to buy
shit we don't even need,
but it's still
just
SHIT!

sometimes
only a vulgarity will serve
to call people's attention
to an impending problem,
which says something about
our faulty cerebellums,
when it takes such a

blunt offense
to shake us out of an
electronic lock-step
right over the brink...

i say "no more."
i have only these words,
so trust me, they will be
well-honed. they will be
cared for. they will be
SHARP.

 what they will NOT be
is inactive
or ignored.

Todd "Grendel" Pack

Stuffed Animals

I wish people
were more like
stuffed animals—
soft, always available
and able to keep secrets—
even the darkest ones.

If you were a
teddy bear,
you wouldn't look at me
and wonder
what went wrong.
You wouldn't judge
or condemn.
You would simply
smile tenderly,
let me hold you
to my chest
and collect my tears
with your plush fur coat.

Maranda Russell

So the Universe Imagines

it's fog but not fog,
seeps between words
between sleep and waking
black at first then gray
hazy gray confusion.

Words jumbled, focus askew,
flashing shrieking stanching stimuli
laborious processing, stabbing pain.

seeking new self
despite denial to accept
missing movement action noise and joy.
New spaces open where old ones are gone,
finding enjoyment there,
when I can.

Weariness beyond darkness,
exhaustion no rest can aid,
day succumbs to night,
night stretches on through wakefulness.

Life's doppelganger, Death, both pinnacles,
the pendulum ignores the in-between
I name Survival.
A destination I'm proud of
yet the toll is high.
It exists but is not life.
It exists in the midst of life.
      (living the other's imagination)

Melissa R. Root

"The Water Drove Her Crazy" by TM Rhyno

Thoughts On Healing.

the hit forces survival and immunity,
the bruise is where you heal,
the rest of the body, however beautiful,
is a wasteland of unused potential.
we do not need the strikers,
but we need the strikes to gain resistance,
inspire adaptation and change.
nothing quite as beautiful as a wound healing,
a broken bone reuniting itself,
a cut sealing,
a body protected by cells.
to heal, we must feel pain,
to survive, we must have a thick skin,
to change, we must hate the place we are in,
and keep on moving.
the hits come from life,
and produce the keys to surviving it.
otherwise, you're dead.

James Barrett Rodehaver

Sensei

Despite the thunder and lightning, we step outside our comfort zone
and notice only the rain...
because we know that if we stay sitting inside, being safe and dry
then we can never wash away those guilty stains.

Years of embitterment, regret, anger... so unbridled and relentless...
barely able to crawl on my bruised, cut knees over broken glass just
to get over to that antique chair...
staring the edges of my minds raindrops through bloody, bloody eyes
that share the look of emotion like an eight hundred pound
silver-back, just screaming at the sunlight and raging skies
and I pound my chest like I pound my cerebral cortex trying to write this out.

My words weigh like dried cement,
heavily by the pound.
I sit here typing words
soon to be recording,
opening those golden doors
towards my way out,
as I rage, rage,
against the intensity of the life.
Burning both ends to find the means and letting it go on like midnight oil,
I make torches out of poetic matchsticks and put my life on display ...
a renaissance represented by wear, tear and strenuous toil.

Any body in this shape would have been toe-tagged by now
but this working body hasn't even begun to fight....
it rises off the floor, wipes off the dirt....
yet keeps the grime.
See, anyone can get knocked out, but those who float like butterflies
don't substitute style for substance
on shuffling their grind.

Busting ass, I feel like I'm bustin' loose,
prior to being Jojo, I don't get back but dance as fast as I can.
I work hard, no apologies. I'm hard, like refined steel
in old-school, New England factories
...bangin' drums like a determined one-man band...
like a number of Texas summers, my steel is driving the mental wheel
not looking for platitudes or ego feeding, festooned platinum record sales,
but to cure ancient, reticent maladies, mental casualties of a war
more biological in terror
more internal, more worse for wear...
cause by years of bullshit I believed
about myself
shoveled down my throat
as prime select.
Did I start to get more select ?
Yes.
To the point that the truth became its own, unique dialect.
My rhymes are meant to be like insulin to a diabetic,
just a cure for tons of manure ...
past, diseased misconceptions dressed up like gangster couture.
No. I'm looking to raise the library,
house partyin' with Rollins, Burroughs, and Dostoyevsky.
Turning intellectualism into prime A-grade sensuality,
by any means sensibly,
is to me a no-brainer for my mental facilities.
This is a spoken word feast,
a vocabulary banquet brought to be feasted,
courtesy of a copy machine,
cut and paste literary Machiavelli.

Any body in this shape would have been toe-tagged by now
but this working body hasn't even begun to fight....
it rises off the floor, wipes off the dirt....
yet keeps the grime.

See, anyone can get knocked out, but those who float like butterflies
don't substitute style for substance
on shuffling their grind.

Digging a quarry of rockin' anthems, rollin' vowels and consonants like
attending a seedy bar with cheap cigarette smoke, 70's Southern rock,
worn out felt on pool tables and no cover tab,
I'm Bookmark(y) McFly, 88 miles per hour
lore an' aural conjugal visits,
whisperin' woo
in my young MILF's ear
and crashin' the prom
with Chuck Berry riffs,
while all the while I'm Piven-iting cute quips
like a Cupidic arrow stab.
It's like a Bromeley's quandary strip mined,
redefining old text with new heat.
It's warmed up in waves
so your 7 pounds
dine on words
that are ready to eat.

Any body in this shape would have been toe-tagged by now
but this working body hasn't even begun to fight....
it rises off the floor, wipes off the dirt....
yet keeps the grime.
See, anyone can get knocked out, but those who float like butterflies
don't substitute style for substance
on shuffling their grind.

the only explosive elements I am around
are found in a dictionary,
all dog-earred with encouragement and determination
...such is the bravery
of the fearless

hunters and gatherers from within
supplemented by substance,
without cheap contents
and giving shout outs like jello shots to the working class,
all the while winking with that certain twinkle
in the ever present third eye.
I let myself finally smile, showing the lines that crinkle.
I nod, pulling out old, well-worn tomes
like much respected friends
and look for some new spoken word testament
that is prophetic,
prolific,
personable....
new world vestals,
without having to rob Pete to pay Paul
but rather speaking out a heartfelt response and call...
Shall I stop ? Never. It is better to die with the words
printed firmly in the air then to live and let those words
never be committed to history.... I rob no human their words
and I certainly am no poem cop.
I may appear as culturally blank as Canadian snow on the
ground, but in me you eventually will
find a diamond if you know
what you seek.

Any body in this shape would have been toe-tagged by now
but this working body hasn't even begun to fight....
it rises off the floor, wipes off the dirt....
yet keeps the grime.
See, anyone can get knocked out, but those who float like butterflies
don't substitute style for substance
on shuffling their grind.

Coyote Wiley

Silence is Disturbing

Silence is disturbing like children have wings.
— John Dawson Beard

i trace the thorny languages
from places i've never seen, and
in the voids between the words
are rhythmic sounds
of drums, of gunfire, of breaths
gasped in desperation
between one wretched hovel to the next.
We are not there,
yet. We breathe the smoke
of distant crematoriams, and
we craft ornate denials
to ward off the inevitable,
a futile apophasis.

Our children are going to hold us
accountable. We have
clipped the wings of angels,
twisted their faces awry like gargoyles,
and taught them to mock
any culture that does not embrace
the lifestyle we've grown complacent in.
We do not want them to succeed,
because in our dark hearts,
their success means our failure,
that they have grown beyond us,
that they might create something
different . . . .
as it is now in other nations
who strive to quell the uprising of the youth,

so it shall be with us.
This is no mere speculation, but
a prophecy written ages ago
translated by a great dreamer
in Babylonian captivity:
our measure has been taken,
and we are found wanting.

empires always crumble; machines always fail.
we have placed the tools of our unmaking
into the bitter hands of tomorrow
that will not look kindly on us
as we utterly fail again. what happens
to a world full of vampires
when there are no living creatures left
to feed the thirst for blood?
the last of the living refuse
the undead embrace, and instead
will leave us to perish
in the pyres we've created
assuring them they were for
the burning of others, though
they have already felt the heat
and been singed
as the multiplicity of infernos
has blazed out of control.

"Children should be seen, not heard,"
a mantra of a Victorian past
that has grown like a tumor on our hearts,
and now more blood feeds the illusion
than our brains.
The silence is going to be shattered
by pounding drums of revolutionary hearts;
we have created the perfect alembic

and unknowingly mixed the explosive chemicals
in the precise proportions
to create this.

They will not hold still to let their wings be clipped.
They will not listen to the double-tongued speeches.
And they will not be silent
much longer.
The momentary pause, the indrawn breath,
is a disturbing silence,
causing a frightened elite
to frantically construct legislation
that only applies
to the voices they know
will break the silence.

I know of a Force that repairs broken angels,
and a Champion who chooses His troops
from the legions of the oppressed, rejected, and ignored.
Who among us have suffered the worst
as we've flailed about? Who have
been caught between the crushing forces
of hypocrisy?
You will not stave off this uprising
by continuing to deny it, by
continuing to deprive it, by
trying to starve it to death.
Your demise has not been revoked,
it has only been postponed.

Todd "Grendel" Pack

All There Is.

On her breath, an apology waiting to happen
Growing behind happy seduction
Beastly fears feed on themselves
And she dances alone with her memories

Nothing waits to change; she moves
Potentials scored into toe-print swirls
Undulations challenge dirt to rise like dough
And cloud like smoke and ashes at her ankles

Her heart beats restart, and restart, and restart
From the edge and at the center
Weaving and leaping in unconscious direction
To wind both in and out like motionless spirals

Healing became a fresh face pointed forward
As avenues sprang up from granite
Like hundred-year-old tombstone memorials
Still telling a bright diary where ends begin

But doubt continues; pause before condolence
Enjoying the swirling passionate moments
Coated in shadow, she is also the light
And the dance is all there is—
to lose

Terri Richardson

Yawn, It's Going To Be A Long Day

Waking up to the realization
today is going to be the last
in a long string which began
at birth is said to be refreshing;
food tastes better than ever,
steps do not drag in heavy air,
are easier to take in that drive
to the finish line (ask a runner),
birds chirping calls translated
into greeting pleasantries for
soon to be newfound brethren
of flight.

Jumping off a cliff is an easy out
when no parachute available
means more than there is not
one lying around; wouldn't help
anyway, the pull cord is broken
(might as well be) and safety
hell... don't discount end goals
shaped like targeted hard soil,
it tastes best ingested at speeds
approaching or exceeding gravity.

A piece of sand inside chowder
will not ruin any sort of mood
on this, the finest of final days;
it serves as a reminder, teeth
never have to be brushed again!

White shining smile or decay
does not matter so why not
show them off to every stranger
contacted on that forever walk;
seafood breath may be ugly,
but true joy should never hide
because of its effect on others...
beautiful the way they beam
while returning misinterpreted
friendly waves.

Confidence replacing common
humdrum, maybe this is how
habits start; a little positive
reinforcement has never hurt
anybody. Unplanned skipping
just sort of happens on the way
and before considering why,
the course undergoes a bit of
a change. After an active, happy
day, it sounds like a better ending
to wind up between the sheets
again, open eyes tomorrow
and hit play.

Travis Laurence Naught

Mirrors

We are beginning to resemble the civilized ones
that came in a chorus of rape
and built strange towers.
We are ingesting their toxic communions,
planting their mutant seeds that choke out
the sage and yellow flowers.

Curse them,
curse them one by one.
Do not marry them.
If he lays you down
poison his morning cup
in the name of our fathers,
our brothers who died-
Allow no children
to be born alive.

The woman of this tribe
will be slaves to no one.
Our women have souls.
Our women have minds.
We are the keepers of memory,
the mirrors of paradise.
We remember a time when
we were naked and unashamed.
We worked our magic
in the open eye of the moon.
Our men were guardians
of the sacred blood and womb.
We danced and feasted with
horned and feathered spirits.
Never forget to teach our daughters—

as civilized man comes intent to
kill the last of our people
by degrading and polluting her spirit-
You, daughter, are worth more
than a thousand blue-eyed beasts.
You, daughter, are the last warrior standing.
You, daughter, are our priestess.

Trier Ward

Exercise

6:30 am.
Wake up
sit up
Coffee's hot
drink up
get going
start moving
sit down
check the mail
read the message
stand up
sit down
check hulu
nothing new
pick out clothes
hit the shower
look at destiny
still sleepin away
what a day
7:30am
shower time
waters hot
soak it up
7:50am
get dressed
fix hair
look at destiny
envy her life without stress
sleeps 20 hrs a day
7:55am
leave for work
8:10am

work is work
not the dream job
ok let loose
no deadlines today
no work to be done
time to work on self
move forward
make a plan
take a stand for my life
resort to blogging.......
9am
free writing exercise not going so well
this isn't impressive
this is crap
just let go
relax
think for yourself
enjoy the envies, the crazies,
the ugliness
wordsies
new old jack be nimble jack be quick
inspire this would be writer to say something other then a
journalistic rata-tat-tat of
woeful woes and
I'm on a bus
bus is in a tunnel
millions of people standing smashed against the sides of
the bus
bus is moving
people dance to avoid being ran over
bus driver speeds up, the people cry out
i scream " dammit Sam slow down, you're killing them"
Sam just turns and slaps me back into my seat
mean ass bus driver
where's he driving me?

where are we going?
why am i on the bus?
Why are we in a tunnel?
the morning comes and no ones left
the bus is abandoned
I awake and crawl out
a new world awaits
cryptic
desolate
empty
the air is enchanting
I can feel it
something lies over the horizon
dare i go to investigate
of course i do
a gypsy on the road
and toad in the sand
the desert is white
the sky is red
an angel cries out
"death is amongst us all"
i invite her in
the bungalow is wearing a shaw
the shaw has a name of george
bernard is his second
he wrote of man and superman
i've never read that story
the buried come back
the demon lays black
you think i'm crazy
i'm forced to agree
now lets us dance along this nightly investigative research
of something new or nothing
here's to you and i and all of us who still read along these lines and
as they continually pass through my mind and leave my finger tips

a taste is all i get
i'm typing fast as hell right now
i'll look back in a few days and not know how these words came to be
but i'll look forward to trying to duplicate the feeling i have right now
dare you try the same
YOU MUST
it feels great
let go
breathe the fire
taste the water
my belly aches with incarnations of the gods
the ancients
the ruins lye bleeding with sacrifices for us to find
will you travel with me
shall we go
theres the road
i take this time to jump on down it
the road is long
the year is new
2010
time to begin
time is short
heart attack in the middle of the night
could rip me from this world
not YET!
too much life unsung
too many songs unlived
never will i know what it means to have been
till i have done everything that burns within
this should be true for all men
if i never climb a mountain
then ill have at least made for myself a fountain of words
meaningless and silently meaningful for those eyes bright enough
to decrypt the obvious hints of self deluded independence
davinci was an animal

a man beast of creation

the first respected man to have what some now call A.D.D.

and he used it well!

i call it the artists curse for we all share a common ground

curiouser and curiouser as the night grows down and the wealth of dreams abound

we open our minds to everything

and everything opens itself to us.

some of us have difficulty breathing these days

this is because we can no longer see the stars

Last time i saw the stars i could see my thoughts for miles and the words spilled out

sometimes 80 pages or more a month. sometimes 10 a pages a day...

written thought over thought explained unexplained

i disguise my messages to myself I add in words to distract the rest of you

but if you should find something of meaning hidden within this callous hide.

then good for you at least its not all for nothing

I go back to destiny

eats as soon as she wakes

runs

tears my shit up

hides

scampers

jumps

licks my toes

no more woes

destiny has vanished

shes sleeping somewhere else

ill venture to find her later

i feel bad for men who consistently say the phrase " I wouldn't venture to say but..."

damnit man.. youre a man

you call yourself such right

then by all means venture to say it if you think it

even if you assume it

i dare the accused to change my mind and prove me wrong. do not be timid in this world for this is not a timid world you either take shit or you throw it. if someone throws shit your way you have two options either throw it back and may the best

turd tosser win or let it build up then you when their guard is down
you pick them up and toss them into the pile they have helped to create.
that makes no sense
or does it
you decide
just listen to the first point.. dont take shit
on another note
why do the rocks in death valley move on their own?
even the ones that weigh up to 2 tons?
I think it's because God plays games like Back Gammon, and the
Chinese game GO
what do you think?

WC Chambers

In the Flames

A Samurai sword does not gain its beauty
Until it is tempered with fire and water
Folded many times within the heat, the flames
It grows stronger and more beautiful
For its time spent in the flames

A glorious vase begins with an inspired thought
It turns upon the wheel many times
Beloved, caressed, adorned
But its beauty and strength come only in the end
When it is changed, solidified by time spent
In the flames, the fires of creation
It is not complete until it survives the change, becoming
Stronger and more beautiful
By enduring the heat, the fire
For its time spent in the flames

A forest goes through seasons of growth and change
Seasons of sunshine, storm, and fire
After its time of decimation, of endings, of weathering the flames
New growth emerges
Stronger and more beautiful
For its time spent in the flames

The Phoenix lives a full life
But does not learn about rebirth
Does not know that it will face
Trials of tempering and change
Born anew with strength and beauty
Until its time spent in the flames
And from the ashes
A glorious new being emerges,

Rising holy, new and true, remade
Stronger and more beautiful
For its time spent in the flames

And like the Phoenix, man is born
Potential for greatness grows within
A seed that craves
The sun and rain and storms
Who does not know his power
Or what he could become
Until the day he's tried and formed
Stepping deep into the flames
No survival guaranteed
Emerging different, more alive
Stronger and more beautiful
For his time spent in the flames

S. Wallace

Opposite: "Set Free" by Claire Ibarra

#aboutthesurvivors
#editors

Born on life support and still alive despite the odds,

James Barrett Rodehaver,

also known as "Bear," to those who know him, is a happily married 31-year old poet, author, and editor living with his husband in Dallas, Texas. A native of Alabama, He is a survivor of many things, ranging from health problems that required up to six different surgeries to an abusive and tumultuous childhood growing up. James has written poetry since he was seven years old, and his indomitable spirit shows through in his poetry, and touches many lives. James frequents the Dallas open mic scene, most notably Mad Swirl, a popular monthly open mic hosted by Chicago native Johnny Olson. He has written a book of poetry called *Strangely Wonderful*, published by Penhall Publishing, who now uses his services as an editor. James has a true passion about books, poetry, and helping make people's literary dreams come true.

Poems:

battleground.	127
i love you like burning churches still pray...	28
It's Gonna Hurt.	271
I've lived in that house.	60
Ode To Tortured Artist.	231
Thoughts On Healing.	280

Almost dead at birth,

Lilly Penhall

was born to be a survivor. Her first poem was published at age 8 and she started writing for stage and screen shortly thereafter. After earning a bachelor's degree in creative writing in 2003, she quit writing for several years before being led to the open mic scene in Dallas, Texas, which reignited her love of words. Lilly has been published in The Dallas Morning News, *Forces Literary Magazine* (Collin College), *Beatest State of the Union* (Slough Press), *Every Reason 'Zine, Kleft Jaw, madswirl.com*, and was featured on the Live @ Lost Art Open Mic CD (PAO Productions), in addition to publishing her own poetry collection, *O*, a collaboration with photographer Rosie Lindsey, and co-editing *Let It Bleed* femme zine. Through her family's company Penhall Publishing and her own Interstellar Graphics, she has found her calling in book design and publishing. In 2012, she relocated to beautiful San Diego, California, where she works from home as a book designer so she can take care of her new baby.

Poems:

Scars	122
Today	170

#contributors

Gayle Bell's

work has been featured in a number of anthologies. In 2013-2014, she was a Co-Exhibitor for My Immovable Truth—A Dallas Lineage put on by MAP (Make Art With Purpose). She facilitated her and other GLBTQY's oral history and performances.

Poem:

Open Letter: I Will Rename Us   160

Eric Blackerby

is a 31 year old equipment operator who lives with his wife Amber in Birmingham, Alabama. He has a love for the Alabama Crimson Tide that borders on the inappropriate, and is an eclectic music lover, with country music being his favorite. He has written poetry in the past, but currently his focus is being a singer-songwriter, and he also writes a sports blog about Alabama football entitled Saban's Sidewalk. He has a big heart and an even bigger laugh. He has survived many hardships during his life, but always comes out smiling, and stronger than before.

Poems:

Far Away.   115
Five Years.   196
Night Roaming.   222

Terri Black,

a practicing writer, teacher and avid swimmer, has been writing since 2009. A lifelong native of Oklahoma City, she earned her Bachelor of Arts degree from the University of Central Oklahoma and is currently studying for her Masters in Creative Writing. Her short story, Dream Chasing in Colorado was published in *The Absolute*, an Oklahoma City Community College publication in 2009. After the Moore, May 20, 2013 tornado, her article "Courage: A Moore Teacher's Story of Survival," was published in the Oklahoma Observer. She is currently writing a fictional novel and her memoir.

Poem:
Desecrated   180

Justin Booth

is something of a rising star in the small literary world of Central Arkansas. Raised in Northeast Arkansas, Booth is a veteran of the U.S. Army who worked as a bricklayer, rode with a motorcycle gang, and did time in prison before falling into heroin addiction that eventually left him homeless on the streets of Little Rock for more than five years. In all that time, writing was his salvation and what carried him through. Since the publication of his first poetry chapbook, "Hookers, Ex-Wives and Other Lovers," in 2012, he has found a job and a home, left the streets, and has seen his work published in magazines and anthologies both in the U.S. and abroad. In 2013 he released *Trailer Park Troubadour*, and his latest collection *Lucky Strikes, Grave Dirt, and 1/3 of the Stars* is available on Amazon.com. Booth lives and works in Little Rock.

Poems:
Move Slow	149
Summers	228
They Sicken	262
This One Thing I Pray	207

Heather M. Browne

is a faith-based psychotherapist and recently emerged poet, published in the *Orange Room, Boston Literary Review, Page & Spine, Eunoia Review, Poetry Quarterly, The Poetry Bus, Red Fez, The Muse, An International Journal of Poetry, Deep Water Literary Journal, Electric Windmill, Maelstrom, mad swirl*, and *Dual Coast*. Her first chapbook, *We Look for Magic and Feed the Hungry* has been published by MCI. She just won the Nantucket Poetry Competition. She has been married 20 years to her love, has 2 amazing teens, and can be found frolicking in the waves. Follow her: www.thehealedheart.net.

Poems:

Our Penny	98
Scrubbing	58
Unboxed	55
You Take From Me	88

Allison Bruning

is the bestselling author of several historical fiction books. She holds a MFA in Creative Writing from Full Sail University and a BA in Theater Arts from Sul Ross State University in Alpine, Texas. Allison's hobbies include hiking, camping, reading, visiting museums, and traveling with her husband. She is a screenwriter, author and scriptwriter from Marion, Ohio but lives in Indianapolis, Indiana.

Poems:

The Phoenix	258
Twisting and Turning	77

Tavis P. Brunson

is a poet, minister, writer and playwright. Originally from Columbia, SC, he has performed and taught across the United States. He's been published in several anthologies and currently working on 2 poetry collections and a novel. A national and regional poetry slam champion, he's also done many projects with Billy Graham Evangelistic Association in Charlotte, NC. He has fabulous hair.

Poems:

Monster	184
Spiraling	103
Unopened Letter	244

Wes Chambers

is a Wolf man; born in a desperate land where buzzards swarm red skies and the only thing louder than the mating call of the coyotes is the native tribal songs of the Indian nation. Where circus music plays like swirling madness around fools and kings... or, rather in Oklahoma. He spends his days in Dallas, TX doing 3D Architectural visualization, making a daily attempt to approach practical life with the mad heart spirit of a poet. His howl can be heard for miles.

Poems:

Exercise	293
Static	90
Troubles	129

What's not to love? If there were a prize for sincere humility,

Susan Dobbe Chase

would win it, hands down. No one would feel upset or jealous because she's so humbly fantastic that she would glance at them and they would fall in love with her. Everyone does. If she weren't so amazing, she'd probably find it annoying. However, she's accustomed to people going gaga over her. That's just one of her many charms.

Poem:

For Andreas   68

PW Covington

has been a fixture in the Texas poetry scene since the late 1990's. His work has been published by University of Texas Pan American, Our Lady of the Lake University, and South Texas College. Covington is a veteran of two wars, has served time inside the Texas state prison system, and is active in humanitarian and disaster relief operations. PW lives in rural Lavaca county Texas with his English Bulldog, Chesty, and he tends family ranch land near Cuero. His recently released novel, *Dear Elsa,* can be ordered from your favorite Indie book seller.

Poems:

Recidivists   241
Short Final (Somalia 1992-93)   86
The Last Time That The World Ended   75

Helen Coy-Gresavage

is a native of Nanjemoy, Maryland, and has been writing poetry since high school. While earning her Bachelor's Degree in Theater and Dance at St. Mary's College of Maryland, she founded the St. Mary's Spoken Poets club, and performed in events on and off campus. Helen has a passion for performance in all forms, and has been performing burlesque in the DC/Baltimore area for three years under the stage name Faith Grenade. Helen currently lives in Kanagawa, Japan with her husband, Justin and two beloved ferrets, Faye and Onyx.

Poem:
Cripple   229

Logen Cure

is a poet and teacher. She is the author of a chapbook, In Keeping, published by Unicorn Press in 2008. Her work also appears in *Word Riot, Cactus Heart, IndieFeed: Performance Poetry*, and elsewhere. She earned her MFA in Creative Writing from the University of North Carolina at Greensboro. She lives in Grand Prairie, Texas with her wife. Learn more at www.logencure.com.

Poems:
I'll be out in a minute.   236
Jock Dates Drummer.   168
May.   221

Adam Eason

is a mostly-musician, and a sometimes-poet. He goes around the Greater Dallas Metroplex teaching people of all stripes how to wrangle cello strings, and then writes poetry when he gets the chance. Also, he writes music from time to time. Generally, though, he tries to spend as much time sleeping as possible, as that truly is the best of all possible worlds, despite what that fool Dr. Pangloss would have you believe.

Poem:

Pyrrhic Victory   34

Lori Lasseter Hamilton

is a ten-year breast cancer survivor and at night, she works as a medical records clerk. She has competed in the Montevallo Poetry Slam since 2003. In 1996, she was almost arrested at Birmingham's City Stages Spoken Word Festival for using profanity in her poem. Lori earned a Bachelor of Arts in journalism from UAB and from 2011 to 2012, she was a freelance writer for *Birmingham Weekly*. *Fester* and Staplegun Press have published her poems, and New Dawn Unlimited published her first poetry chapbook, *live, from the emergency room*. She is married to Robert Hamilton.

Poems:

Breast monologue   118
pretty in pink   133
Welcome to the show   124

Jennifer E. Hudgens,

originally from Oklahoma City, has been previously published in *Kill Poet, Decomp, Pedestal, Requiem, Divine Carcass, Artistica Magazines,* & Swimming With Elephants Publications Anthology *Light as a Feather* (2014). She has released several poetry chapbooks including; *1729* in 2012, *For the Ghosts We Were* and *The Secret Lives of Harriet Turbine* in 2014. She has also been featured on Indiefeed Performance Poetry, and a guest poet at Oklahoma's H&8th Market night as a Short Order Poet. Jennifer is Co-Editor of Wicked Banshee Press, founder of The Oklahoma Poetry Events Page on facebook, is organizer of a weekly workshop series in OKC. Jen is currently pursuing her Bachelor's degree in Creative Writing at the University of Central Oklahoma. Jennifer watches the sky the way most people watch television. She has an unmatched passion for poetry and life. She is obsessed with cheese, loves unicorns. She is terrified of clowns and horses. She also hates talking about herself in third person. See more at Charliewortham.tumblr.com, Shortorderpoems. tumblr.com, and Soundcloud.com/thehudgepoetry.

Poems:

Any good.	123
Autopsy.	20
Dribble, Deities Haunt Hallways.	26
Metal Dragon.	30
No.	163
On Instinct: Found Love notes	99
Scar-light.	120
Sweet Waltz.	116
Whiskey Psalm.	235

Jerri Hardesty

lives in the woods of Alabama with husband, Kirk, also a poet. They run the nonprofit organization, NewDawnUnlimited, Inc., dedicated to poetry publishing, production, performance, promotion, preservation, and education. This includes organizing and hosting the BamaSlam Montevallo Poetry Slam in Montevallo, Alabama, as well as other NDU and BamaSlam poetry events around the state. Jerri has had over 300 poems published, and has won more than 600 awards and titles in both written and spoken word/performance poetry at the local, regional, national, and international level. Find out more at NewDawnUnlimited.com.

Poems:

A Perfect Storm	158
Beautifully Broken	21
This Poem	165

Claire Ibarra

is photographer residing in Miami, Florida. Her photographs have appeared in numerous journals and magazines, including *SmokeLong Quarterly, Alimentum, Roadside Fiction, Stone Path Review,* and *Blue Fifth Review.* She was a visual-artist-in-residence for Counterexample Poetics and is currently art director for *Gulf Stream Magazine.* Her work was included in the "Finding the Light" Exhibition at PhotoPlace Gallery.

Photos:

"C'est la vie"	100
"Set Free"	300
"Watching Over Me"	58

Known mostly for his constant evolving style,

Christopher Johnson,

without complaint, combines the experience discord of his past, the wisdom of now and the hope of the future to give voice to a universal message of human spark that connects us all. Using the intricate combination of academia, hip hop, traditional storytelling, theater, and just plain old common sense, Christopher provides a soulful uplifting experience to move audiences through several states of equilibrium, challenging listeners not to remain emotionally stagnant. Currently residing in Providence, Rhode Island, he organizes spoken word events, gives workshops on writing, performing, as well as growth and empowerment through words.

Poems:

Broken Mends	49
forgiveness	144
Monsters	215
Untitled "I am broken water"	259

Paul Koniecki

lives in Fort Worth, Texas. He is on staff at Mad Swirl and as a man of few words and many poems. His work has appeared in places such as *Kleft Jaw, Red Fez, Windy Hill Review, Illya's Honey, Red River Review, Mad Swirl*, and many more. Mostly he likes to whisper lines to strangers and run.

Photo by Rosie Lindsey

Poems:

a million kisses and a comet's tail to the edge of the milky way	127
Coming Early	225
Connect the Wild Dots	83
Ode to Cut	248
Silent Dog	64
take your seat please/playground marbles	174

Stephen Lawson

was born on May 2nd, 1970 to a military father and hippie mother in Honolulu, Hawaii while his dad was in Vietnam. He was passed from mom to dad and various relatives due to overseas duty and divorce. Lawson proudly says he raised himself, in every juvenile facility and group home in 1980's Oklahoma. He joined the US Army as a Stinger gunner and infantryman in the 25th Infantry (Light) in—of all places—Hawaii. He returned home to drug addiction and criminal enterprise... and eventually landed in prison. He started writing after a mid-life crisis and found Red Dirt Poetry online after an internet search and going to their Wednesday open mic in November 2011. When not writing or performing, Stephen can be found playing hackysack, juggling, riding his unicycle, and wooing redhead women.

Poem:
"Ours is not to wonder why..."   81

Grant Leuning

is a poet and essayist in San Diego, California. He has had work in published in *The New Inquiry, TINGE, Kapsula Magazine* and *Three Word Chant*. He is the co-author, with designer Eric Carlson, of two zines of speculative poetry, *Sentence and Aliquid Quo Nihil Maius Cogitari Possit*, and published his first collection of poems, *I Don't Want To Die in the Ocean* in 2012. Currently, he is the organizer of the San Diego reading series NOW! That's What I Call Poetry and is putting together his second collection, *Empty Bird*. He writes at twitter and tumblr as IllllllllllllllI.

Poem:
Ape Bite   162

Rosie Lindsey,

a breast cancer survivor, is a native born Texan that spent family vacations exploring the back roads of the southwest. She grew up in the days of drive-in movies and restaurants, freak shows at the state fair and neon advertising, experiences which have shaped her art. She's interested in the ghosts of the past and travel with an eye for capturing people and landscapes that will soon disappear. Current projects include Back Roads of Texas, Big Momma and Cancer Stick.

Photos:

"Smoking Woman with Ford"	38, Cover
"Saw"	18
"Alive: World's Most Amazing Show"	125
"Head Behind a Rock"	135
"Cancer Stick"	173
"Zombies"	223

Agnes Marton

is a Hungarian-born poet and Reviews Editor at The Ofi Press. Recent publications include *Estuary: A Confluence of Art and Poetry* (USA, got the Saboteur Award as Best Mixed Anthology); *Drifting Down the Lane* (USA); *Glitter is a Gender* (UK). She has been in collaboration with artist Midori McCabe. Dan Chappell wrote music for one of her poems, it was performed by the BBC Singers. 'Guardian of the Edge', her forthcoming poetry exhibition (scheduled for November, 2014, Luxembourg) is going to showcase artworks by forty international artists, all inspired by her poetry.

Poems:

Exposed	97
Travelmarvel	255

Travis Laurence Naught

is an author who happens to be a quadriplegic wheelchair user. *The Virgin Journals* (ASD Publishing, 2012) and *Still Journaling* (e-book, 2013) are full-length collections of his confessional style poetry. Travis has had individual pieces of his writing appear widely online (*Deadman's Reach, Empty Sink Publishing, Kind of a Hurricane Press*, etc.) and in print (*Empirical Magazine, Falling Star Magazine, Lost Coast Review*, etc.). Head on over to naughtapoet.blogspot.com to read more of his work and make an online connection!

Poems:

Sick and Tired	36
Yawn, It's Going To Be A Long Day	289

Nero

has been painting for over eight years thanks to her son's curiosity while they were in a dollar store. "It opened my eyes and I saw a person in myself I never knew!" Believing that everyone is an artist, Nero's company, SaturatedArt, encourages all to submit to themselves and create something beautiful. With black as a teacher, Nero used any tool available to achieve things she cannot interpret any other way from her dreams. A poet, artist, writer, and a mom; a woman in her right. See more of her work at saturatedart.wordpress.com.

Paintings:

"Yellow"	44
"Rose"	68
"Red"	72
"Static"	93
"Black"	124
"Blue"	242

Johnny Olson

was born in Chicago. He cut his teeth in the diverse, blue-collared neighborhoods of his hometown. He was reborn in California; where he found himself a new title: United States Marine. After surviving a brief and violent war, he turned in his rifle for a pen and found his passion for writing. In 1998 he got lost and found himself in Dallas. In 1999, Johnny helped start *Mad Swirl*, which has evolved into its own being. After wearing too many hats he now only wears a few at *Mad Swirl*: chief editor, webmaster, and open mic host.

Poem:

Precipitation   154

Todd "Grendel" Pack

is a "white trash wordslinger" who's lived out of the back of an Italian restaurant while running the local Poetry Slam, in a mold-infested illegal Brooklyn basement apartment, and many other places along this poetry trail. He is currently in transition between his hometown of Roanoke, VA to Dallas, TX, where he intends to focus on his poetry, participate in local open mics and slams, and let God write the next chapter of his life. He has participated in Regional and National Slams, and been previously published in *EOTU, Ampersand*, and the local newspaper.

Poems:

Foreword   11
Jericho A.D.   256
Like a Fox   264
O, Beautiful   39
Silence is Disturbing   285
Twist   274

Evan Bryant Patton

is a recent English graduate from the University of Montevallo. He embraces influences from poets such as Wilfred Owen, W.B. Yeats, W.S. Merwin, and Sylvia Plath. With a Muse that has led him through a refreshingly winding path, Evan has found a voice that is equally as visceral, fricative, and heavily engaged with image as it is fluid, flowing, and intellectually complex. He also enjoys referring to himself in the third person, as evidenced by this bio that he has written about himself. If you like what you see, please visit his website at www.evanbryant.weebly.com.

Poems:

Communion	152
Death is not the Problem, Death is the Solution	56
Mother, may I?	32
Old Father, Old Artificer	52

Aparna Pathak

belongs to Delhi, India. Graduate in English (Honors) and post graduate in public relations, her poems have been published in more than 30 print anthologies, online publications and also twice in various literaty magazines like *"Reflections," Negative Suck, Rolling Thunder Press,* and *Blue Cygnus*. One of her poems has been awarded the commendation of " Highly Commended " in the Poem of the Year Category of the Destiny Poets' International Community of Poets ICOP Awards 2012.

Poem:

Absolute Entity	73

Alex Pogosov

was born in Moscow, Russia in 1983. He has lived in Dallas, Texas since 1991, and upon reflection, rather likes it there. He is a writer, an illustrator, and the frontman for the seldom-active band Scarletien. He has hosted the open mic at Bill's Records in three of its incarnations dating back to 2005 (he has attended regularly since 2003). His work has appeared in *Death List Five* (volume 1) and in the *UTD Mercury*, the student newspaper of the University of Texas at Dallas. He also holds a useless art degree from this school.

Poem:

Underwater House   45

Artwork:

"Machete Girl" Drawing   148

Dan Provost's

poetry has appeared in numerous on-line and print magazines. His ninth book, *On the Wagon... On a Binge* was published by What's in the Bag Press. He currently resides in Bellingham, Massachusetts.

Poems:

4:22 AM: Tripping on K-Pins   218
It   230

Ricky A. Pursley

is an award-winning poet and writer currently living in his boyhood hometown of Mattapoisett, Massachusetts. Mr Pursley is a working newspaper reporter who has written over 4,000 poems and a couple dozen short fiction pieces. His poems have appeared in *NoTeS magazine* and *every reason magazine.* His first poetry collection, *Songs from the Road*, will be published soon by Grace Notes Books. He can be reached at rapursley@netscape.net.

Poem:
being supportive   67

TM Rhyno

(The Magic Rhyno) is a freelance artist, illustrator and owner of Magic Rhyno Creative, established in 2006 in DFW metro area. Rhyno is also the 4th official member of the DFW art collective Art-Hunger, a local art chapter that helps promote the arts, makes connections with and for artists, hosts events, fundraisers, showcases and pushes to keep the art local art movement going strong in the heart of the lone star State. For more art and other foolish nonsense or to contact T.M. Rhyno please visit: www.magicrhynocreative.com or visit his facebook fan page at www.facebook.com/MagicRhyno.

Artwork:
"American Justice"   190
"Sanguine Slavery"   96
"Skin Deep"   140
"Skull Study"   31
"The Water Drove Her Crazy"   279

Terri Richardson

is a poet and journalist living in East Texas. She's been writing lines for 20 years, the only thing that's made sense to her to keep at for so long. Professionally, she's been a full-time staff writer and photographer at the Texarkana Gazette and the Marshall News Messenger, also a volunteer at Heliopolis SBC: The underground newspaper of Shreveport/Bossier. A hobbyist poet, her passion for words and relating stories has stained her soul and left ink in her blood.

Poems:

All There Is. 288
Firefighters. 74

Melissa R. Root,

educator, writing adviser, writer, and editor, lives in Denver, CO. She has a PhD in English literary studies and currently teaches at Metropolitan State University of Denver. In January 2012, she sustained a traumatic brain injury in a bicycle accident. Since then, she's been learning to cope with her new reality. She still enjoys reading, biking, hiking, and spending time with her beloved dog Bennie.

Poem:

So the Universe Imagines 278

Maranda Russell

is an award-winning author, artist, poet and cat lover who also happens to have Asperger's Syndrome (a kind of high-functioning autism). She currently lives in Dayton, Ohio with her husband and six cats. For more information about this author or her books/artwork, please visit her website/blog, www.marandarussell.com.

Poems:

Stuffed Animals	277
Suicide Aftermath	169
Wal-Mart Land	19

Artwork:

"Facing the Storm"	78
"Heart Energy"	112

Sharon Sitler

currently lives in western Massachusetts with her adorable and witty eight-year-old son. When she's not procrastinating by reading, gardening, experimenting with new recipes, or tackling various DIY projects, Sharon is working on a collection of poetry that explores the heart wrenching topic of domestic violence and its effects on victims and families. In addition to being a poet, Sharon is a soon-to-be high school English teacher who is currently working on her certification at Westfield State University. Her work has appeared in *Fresh Ink, Big River Poetry Review, Prairie Margins,* and *Paper Nautilus.*

Poems:

Abuse	106
Pawn Shop	33

Rose M. Smith

is an "Air Force brat" poet from Columbus, Ohio's East Side. Her snapshots of the human condition have appeared in magazines, anthologies, and in front of dozens and thousands in live performance. She is author of *Shooting the Strays* (Pavement Saw Press, 2003) and *A Woman You Know* (Pudding House Publications, 2005), co-editor of *Cap City Poets: Columbus and Central Ohio's Best Known, Read, and Requested Poets* (Pudding House Publications, 2008), a Poets' Greatest Hits series (now managed by Kattywompus Press) inductee. Her words to the wise: "It's hard to win prizes with poetry that spans both worlds. You just have to love what you do." Rose is an IT requirements analyst by day and a Cave Canem Fellow all the time.

Poems:

Hangin' at Joe's Hole   27
One-Night Fosters   178

Desmene Statum

moved to Dallas from Alabama in 1999. She attended the Art Institute of Dallas where she studied Interactive Media Design. Not long after moving to Texas, her mentor, Joey Cloudy, exposed her to beat poetry, and she fell in love with the works of Ginsberg and Kerouac. Her biggest literary influence is Octavio Paz, the writer, the revolutionary. She's performed all over the Dallas Metroplex and beyond doing art festivals, writer's workshops, events, and open mics. She has two chapbooks of poetry, *Coagulation*, and *Two Fisted Whiskey Love Songs*. She's been published frequently on *MadSwirl.com* as well as their print edition: *The Blue Note Issue*. She has collaborated with many in the Dallas Poetry Community and favors freestyle duets with friends. Desmene currently resides in Oak Cliff and hopes to publish a collection of her works in June of 2015.

Photo by Tim Thomaston

Poem:

Sometimes a bullet looks pretty good   191

Bekah Steimel

is a 34-year-old, internationally published poet who lives in St. Louis, MO and is working on a first collection of poetry chronicling one lesbian's struggles with addiction, fidelity, mental illness, and mortality. You can find her work in publications such as *Gutter Eloquence, Sinister Wisdom, TRIVIA: Voices of Feminism, Vayavya* and *Verity La*. She was also featured in the Poet Showcase at *Five Magazine*. In addition to poetry, Steimel enjoys writing fiction and is currently working on a novella that explores the themes of love and loss. Visit www.bekahsteimel.com.

Poems:

Untitled I-X   197

Chuck Taylor

is a writer who also loves to take photographs in the fine arts tradition. He has published photographs in his own books and in literary magazines since the 1970's. He teaches at Texas A&M University in College Station. His aim in photography is not to take you away from the world, but to help you see the world in a new way and fall in love again like a child. He enjoys, at times, the presence of little jokes in his photography.

Poem:

Introduction   15

Photo:

"New Growth"   254

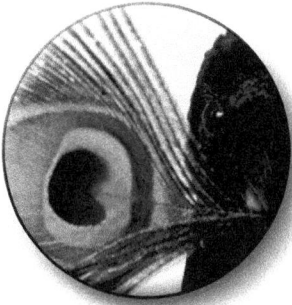

Emma van Woerkom

is a poet and author of the 2013 Heritage Lottery Fund poetry pamphlet *Beside the Seaside*. Her work has been published in magazines, anthologies and music albums. Brought up on the Welsh Marches, she has never been able to sever her ties with this area and spends time shuttlecocking between Somerset and Hay-on-Wye working as a Library Assistant and Shared Reading Facilitator. From an original 1725 high court document in her possession she is researching and writing her second publication, *The Green Canister*, inspired by the life of Teresia Constantia Phillips, London's Notorious 18th Century Courtesan.

Poems:

Deaf Couple	121
Doppler Dreams	270

Victory

is a writer, painter, parent & poet; a graphic designer & copywriter. She's competed in poetry slams against some of the best performance poets in the nation. She has been a member of several Dallas slam teams that traveled to compete at annual National Poetry Slams. In 2004 she was a member of the Dallas Slam team that graced the Finals Stage and took a 3rd place showing at Nationals in St. Louis. She has performed at venues ranging from coffeehouse open mics to schools to radio. Victory's work has appeared in 4 self-published chapbooks as well as on CD & DVD.

Photo by Rosie Lindsey

Poems:

a letter to me from my scar	113
Cry	141
Name	268

Edward Vidaurre

has been been published in several anthologies and literary journals, among them *La Bloga, Bordersenses, Interstice, La Noria Literary Journal, Boundless Anthology* of the Valley International Poetry Festival 2011-2013. He's had two books published: *I Took My Barrio On A Road Trip* (Slough Press 2013) and *Insomnia* (El Zarape Press 2014). He also co-edited *TWENTY-Poems in Memoriam* and *Boundless 2014*, the Anthology of the Rio Grande Valley International Poetry Festival.

Poem:
How to watch me wither   220

S Wallace

lives with two cats by the sea. When Daylight Ends, a book of poetry, was published in 2005, and can be purchased at on line bookstores. Recent publications include *Magic*, a flash fiction story published in *Postcard Poems and Prose Magazine* (April 2014), *Feelings*, an SF short story published by *Former People Journal* in their New Wave SF edition (June 2014), and poetry in *Metaphor Magazine* (June 2014). S Wallace serves on the board of Space Coast Writers Guild and participates in the Cocoa Beach Writers Workshop.

Photo by Suza Goltz

Poem:
In the Flames   299

Trier Ward

is a mother, poet, and scientist. She lives in Pensacola, Florida. Her poetry appears in Rolling Thunder, The Nervous Breakdown, Bohemia, and Mad Swirl. She promotes the spoken and written word, publishes prolifically to a small audience on Facebook, and lives an otherwise private life focused on her children, art, wildlife, and music.

Poems:

Mirrors	291
My Demon	247
Simple Confession	107

The eclectic rhythms of

Yocelin Watts

were derived from an equally diverse background. Born in the Dominican Republic and adopted at the age of three by a loving British couple, Joy and Anthony Watts, she developed a love of linguistics early in life. Now in her early thirties, Yocelin resides in the quiet town of Rollinsford, New Hampshire and despite other artistic outlets, writing still remains a primary facet for emotional release.

Poem:

Attempted Murder of a Love Life	101

Coyote Wiley

was born in Texas. He is a writer. He writes prose and poetry. Everything else is extemporaneous.

Poems:

NYD... WNYL?   238
Sensei   281

Brad Wood

had a wonderful childhood with loving and supportive parents. He spent the middle 15-20 years of his life in some sort of prolonged teenage rebellion. He finally grew up a bit and went back to school to become a nurse. He helps people now with illness, pain, fear, loss, understanding, and a myriad of other ways. Interestingly, he met the love of his life, after he began to be a decent and capable man. They married in the yard of the home they live in now. Brad always wanted to write, like others imagine being firemen at age three and four. The Voice has returned and he's trying to listen now.

Poems:

Amnesia   211
Gainful Employment   192

#Alphabetized

4:22 AM: Tripping on K-Pins	218
Absolute Entity	73
Abuse	106
a letter to me from my scar	113
All There Is.	288
"American Justice"	190
a million kisses and a comet's tail to the edge of the milky way	127
Amnesia	211
Any good.	123
Ape Bite	162
A Perfect Storm	158
Attempted Murder of a Love Life	101
Autopsy.	20
battleground.	117
Beautifully Broken	21
being supportive	67
Breast monologue	118
Broken Mends	49
"C'est la vie"	100
Coming Early	225
Communion	152
Connect the Wild Dots	83
Cripple	229
Cry	141
Deaf Couple	121
Death is not the Problem, Death is the Solution	56
Desecrated	180
Doppler Dreams	270
Drawing: "Machete Girl"	148
Dribble, Deities Haunt Hallways.	26
Exercise	293
Exposed	97
"Facing the Storm"	78

Far Away.	115
Firefighters.	74
Five Years.	196
For Andreas	68
#foreword	11
forgiveness	144
Gainful Employment	192
Hangin' at Joe's Hole	27
"Heart Energy"	112
How to watch me wither	220
I'll be out in a minute.	236
i love you like burning churches still pray...	28
In the Flames	299
It	230
It's Gonna Hurt.	271
I've lived in that house.	60
Jericho A.D.	256
Jock Dates Drummer.	168
Like a Fox	264
May.	221
Metal Dragon.	30
Mirrors	291
Monster	184
Monsters	215
Mother, may I?	32
Move Slow	149
My Demon	247
Name	268
Night Roaming.	222
No.	163
Notes on the Creation of This Anthology	334
NYD... WNYL?	238
O, Beautiful	39
Ode to Cut	248
Ode To Tortured Artist.	231

Old Father, Old Artificer 52

One-Night Fosters 178

On Instinct: Found Love notes 99

Open Letter: I Will Rename Us 160

"Watching Over Me" 59

Our Penny 98

"Ours is not to wonder why…" 81

Painting: "Black" 187

Painting: "Blue" 242

Painting: "Red" 72

Painting: "Rose" 69

Painting: "Static" 93

Painting: "Yellow" 44

Pawn Shop 33

Photo: "Alive: World's Most Amazing Show" 125

Photo: "Cancer Stick" 173

Photo: "Head Behind a Rock" 135

Photo: "New Growth" 254

Photo: "Saw" 18

Photo: "Smoking Woman With Ford" 38

Photo: "Zombies" 223

Precipitation 154

pretty in pink 133

Pyrrhic Victory 34

Recidivists 241

"Sanguine Slavery" 96

Scar-light. 120

Scars 122

Scrubbing 58

Sensei 281

"Set Free" 301

Short Final (Somalia 1992-93) 86

Sick and Tired 36

Silence is Disturbing 285

Silent Dog 64

Simple Confession 107

"Skin Deep" 140

"Skull Study" 31

Sometimes a bullet looks pretty good 191

So the Universe Imagines 278

Spiraling 103

Static 90

Stuffed Animals 277

Suicide Aftermath 169

Summers 228

Sweet Waltz. 116

take your seat please/playground marbles 174

The Last Time That The World Ended 75

The Phoenix 258

"The Water Drove Her Crazy" 279

They Sicken 262

This One Thing I Pray 207

This Poem 165

Thoughts On Healing. 280

Today 170

Travelmarvel 255

Troubles 129

Twist 274

Twisting and Turning 77

Unboxed 55

Underwater House 45

Unopened Letter 244

Untitled 197

Untitled 259

Wal-Mart Land 19

Welcome to the show 124

Whiskey Psalm. 235

Yawn, It's Going To Be A Long Day 289

You Take From Me 88

Notes on the Creation of This Anthology

We put no limit on the number of pieces each author or artist submitted in effort to give everyone a chance to tell their stories. Once we received all the submissions, I sent them to Bear without the author names so that he would truly choose the best poems without bias. Indeed, he chose nine poems by Jennifer Hudgens and six poems by Paul Koniecki without knowing who wrote them. Bear chose the best poems for inclusion and then sent the poems back to me to make the final decisions. For the most part, I chose to include more poems that I think also deserved to be published in our book—which is how it turned into an almost 350 page beast.

We did our best to ensure proper spelling and grammar where we felt the authors would have wanted it, but mostly left each poem as the author stylistically intended. The "hashtagories" as Bear dubbed them, his innovative way of categorizing the chapters, along with the bios written as chat bubbles, are just our way of combining printed books with new technology... love it or hate it. While it may not be perfect, we have put a lot of work into the creation of this anthology as a platform to tell stories of survival and hope that this book gives you a newfound gratitude for your life as it has for us.

I sincerely thank you for reading this book and supporting those brave enough to speak their truth and survive without apology.

Lilly Penhall
Co-Editor

More Titles By Penhall Publishing

All of the following titles are available to purchase at Amazon.com and www.penhallpublishing.com. Visit our website for more information.

———————————

The Jenna Glynn Ghost Stories Series by Vicki Smart Penhall

Strangely Wonderful: Poetry by James Barrett Rodehaver

The Julian Joke, a novel by RT Shoemake

O: Poetry by Lilly Penhall and Photography by Rosie Lindsey

Lies From The Past: A Viet Nam Tale infused with poetry by Vicki Smart Penhall and Wm. Stephen Edwards

Her Papa's House, a short story by RT Shoemake

Coming Soon from Penhall Publishing

The Route of All Evil: Poetry About Vices is accepting submissions of poetry and art until December 31, 2014.

Visit **penhallpublishing.com/books/anthologies** for more information about this and future anthologies to be published by Penhall Publishing, or to submit a theme idea for an upcoming anthology!

www.ingramcontent.com/pod-product-compliance
Lightning Source LLC
Chambersburg PA
CBHW081423090426
42740CB00017B/3158